My Korean: Step 1

The *My Korean* series of textbooks offers a learner-centered, communicative task-based, interactive approach to learning contemporary Korean.

My Korean: Step 1 and *My Korean: Step 2* are arranged thematically around topics that any novice learner of Korean is likely to encounter in their first year of study. Each lesson contains two dialogues showing contemporary Korean in use, followed by succinct grammar and vocabulary explanations.

The focus throughout the books is on communicative in-class activities and tasks that encourage students' active participation. Video clips of the lesson dialogues are available as an online resource, and each unit contains communicative activities based on the dialogue themes.

The engaging structure and communicative approach make *My Korean: Step 1* an ideal text for first-semester Korean courses. It is also a great resource for individual study or one-on-one tutorials on Korean language and culture.

Byung-jin Lim is an associate professor of Korean Language and Linguistics in the Department of Asian Language and Cultures at the University of Wisconsin-Madison (UW-Madison), United States. His areas of interest are phonetics, phonology, second language acquisition, computer-mediated communication, and Korean language textbook development.

Jieun Kim is an adjunct instructor at Christian Life College, United States. She teaches courses in languages, psychology, and education. As an instructor at the University of Wisconsin-Madison, she taught Korean conversational courses and Korean culture. Jieun engages in longitudinal research projects to explore how Korean/English bilingual students construct identities as readers and writers.

Ji-Hye Kim is an associate research fellow at the Korean Educational Development Institute. She earned her PhD in the Department of Curriculum and Instruction at UW-Madison. With a BA in Korean Language and Literature and Education, she taught elementary and advanced level Korean language and literatures at UW-Madison. Her areas of interest are curriculum reforms, teacher education, language, and multicultural issues of immigrant students.

My Korean: Step 1

나의 한국어 "스텝 1"

Byung-jin Lim, Jieun Kim and Ji-Hye Kim

First published 2019
by Routledge
2 Park Square, Milton Park, Abingdon, Oxon OX14 4RN

and by Routledge
52 Vanderbilt Avenue, New York, NY 10017

Routledge is an imprint of the Taylor & Francis Group, an informa business

© 2019 Byung-jin Lim, Jieun Kim and Ji-Hye Kim

The right of Byung-jin Lim, Jieun Kim, and Ji-Hye Kim to be identified as authors of this work has been asserted by them in accordance with sections 77 and 78 of the Copyright, Designs and Patents Act 1988.

All rights reserved. No part of this book may be reprinted or reproduced or utilised in any form or by any electronic, mechanical, or other means, now known or hereafter invented, including photocopying and recording, or in any information storage or retrieval system, without permission in writing from the publishers.

Trademark notice: Product or corporate names may be trademarks or registered trademarks, and are used only for identification and explanation without intent to infringe.

British Library Cataloguing-in-Publication Data
A catalogue record for this book is available from the British Library

Library of Congress Cataloging-in-Publication Data
Names: Lim, Byung-jin, author. I Kim, Jieun, author. I Kim, Ji-Hye, author.
Title: 880-01 My Korean. Step 1 = 나의 한국어. 스텝 1. Sut'ep 1 / Byung-jin Lim,
     Jieun Kim and Ji-Hye Kim.
Other titles: 나의 한국어. 스텝 1
Description: Abingdon, Oxon ; New York, NY : Routledge, 2019. I Includes
     bibliographical references and index.
Identifiers: LCCN 2018041548 I ISBN 9781138659209 (hardback : alk. paper) I
     ISBN 9781138659230 (paperback : alk. paper) I ISBN 9781315620367 (ebook : alk. paper)
Subjects: LCSH: Korean language—Textbooks for foreign speakers—English.
Classification: LCC PL913 .L56 2019 I DDC 495.7/82421—dc23
LC record available at https://lccn.loc.gov/2018041548

ISBN: 978-1-138-65920-9 (hbk)
ISBN: 978-1-138-65923-0 (pbk)
ISBN: 978-1-315-62036-7 (ebk)

Typeset in Sabon and Frutiger
by Apex CoVantage, LLC

Visit the eResources: www.routledge.com/9781138659230

Contents

Part 1		**1**
	Introduction	3
	About this Korean language textbook	3
	Structure of the textbook	4
	Cast of characters	5
	How to use this book	6
	Outline of the book	7
	Preparation	11
	Mastering the Korean alphabet, *Hangeul*	11
Part 2		**27**
1	Greetings 인사	29
2	Meals and foods 식사와 음식	45
3	School life 학교 생활	65
4	Dating 데이트하기	81
Part 3		**99**
5	Weather and health 날씨와 건강	101
6	Thanksgiving Day and Chuseok 추수감사절과 추석	117
7	Korean markets and college clubs/student organizations 한인 마트와 대학 동아리	139
8	Studying Korean 한국어 공부하기	161
	Index	177

Part 1

Contents

- Introduction
- Outline of the book
- Preparation

Introduction

About this Korean language textbook

My Korean: Step 1 is an elementary contemporary Korean language and culture textbook designed for true-beginner Korean language students at the college level in the United States as well as worldwide. The book is designed for formal classroom settings that value student-centered, interactive learning. However, it could also be used with individuals or in one-on-one tutorials of Korean language and culture.

Most Korean language textbooks contain dialogues and contexts where the learners of Korean are assumed to be learning the Korean language and culture while they are living in South Korea. However, given the reality that not all learners of Korean are actually studying in South Korea, many of them find it difficult to relate to the contents in these textbooks. While many students throughout the world enjoy studying Korean language and culture, many will not visit South Korea, and even fewer will live there for an extended period of time. With these students' needs in mind, the authors write this new Korean language textbook with the following features:

- Student-centered themes with contemporary Korean in use
- Communicative culture-based activities
- Straightforward explanations of grammar and new expressions
- Designs for user-friendly and optimal content delivery
- Basic as well as extended vocabulary with Chinese characters
- Companion website featuring multimedia learning tools

1 The current Korean language textbook offers student-centered themes with authentic Korean. From the beginning of the development of the Korean language textbook, students at the authors' institution participated by expressing their thoughts and needs through questionnaires. Their active participation and input became the basis for the themes in each lesson of the book.
2 Each lesson in the book includes two communicative culture-based activities to help students achieve proficiency in the Korean language and culture via active interaction with other students in and outside the classroom.

Part 1

3 The book offers simple and straightforward explanations of grammatical features and new expressions along with sample dialogues to illustrate each grammar point.

4 The book is designed with user-friendliness in mind in order to provide optimal learning opportunities for both students and teachers. For example, bigger fonts are used in Lesson 1 while smaller fonts are utilized in later chapters; pages are organized such that students can easily recognize repeated features; colors are selected for readability and aesthetic balance; and English translations of each dialogue are presented adjacent to the dialogues in early chapters while they are deliberately placed at the end for later chapters.

5 In response to the growing presence of Chinese-speaking learners of Korean in the world, the book also offers vocabulary (basic or extended) with English glosses along with corresponding Chinese characters for those students (e. g., 일, 이, 삼 . . . one, two, three . . . 一, 二, 三 . . .).

6 A companion website has been developed with interactive multimedia materials for all of the dialogues in the textbook.

Structure of the textbook

The textbook contains six main components for each lesson: Dialogues, Grammar and Expressions, Vocabulary, Activities, Cultural Notes, and English Translations.

1 **Dialogues**: Written in contemporary Standard Korean, dialogues provide contexts in which beginning learners of Korean encounter everyday circumstances with their classmates, friends, and instructors from day one at college. Dialogues also present various scenes and contexts where the learners may experience authentic interactions with native speakers of Korean. Students may find it useful to memorize dialogues as they are likely to face them for daily activities in contemporary Korean.

2 **Grammar and expressions**: Grammar used in the dialogues in each lesson is explained in detail using simple and straightforward language. For easy grammar explanation, technical linguistic terminology is deliberately avoided. Instead, simple and detailed explanation is provided for each grammar point for true beginner learners of Korean. Also, new expressions are explained with ample example sentences such that learners can easily study them on their own. At the end of each grammar point, individual practices are also provided. Later chapters (in Part 3) also provide exercises that are based on the explanations of grammar and new expressions. Students are expected to read the "Grammar and Expressions" sections before they come to class.

3 **Vocabulary (basic and expanded)**: Each lesson contains basic and expanded vocabulary. Basic vocabulary is used in the dialogues, and expanded vocabulary consists of additionally recommended words that can be further built onto the basic vocabulary. For successful learning, students are expected to study both basic and expanded vocabulary before each lesson is discussed in the classroom.

4 **Activities**: One of the distinguishing features of the textbook is the inclusion of culture-based activities in each lesson. Specifically, through activities, students can compare and reflect on Korean culture as well as their own culture. In addition, each activity revolves around the themes discussed in the dialogues of each chapter.

5 **Cultural notes**: Culture is an important part of learning any new language, and this textbook offers a unique perspective on Korean culture that many learners of Korean are anxious to learn more about. While reading through these cultural notes, students will experience firsthand the rich and diverse culture found in Korea.

4

Introduction

6 **English translations**: Another distinguishing feature of this textbook is the way in which English translations of the dialogues are provided. For the efficacy of optimal learning of a new language at the beginner level, English translations are provided right next to the dialogues for earlier chapters, while as learners' Korean proficiency grow, English translations are deliberately placed at the end of lesson for later chapters.

Cast of characters

In the textbook, there are two main characters, **Rachel** and **Yoon-ho**. Rachel is a female American student who has a deep interest in Korean popular culture and Yoon-ho is a male Korean student who studies at a US college. The conversation between the two begins when they meet at Student Orientation.

Yoon-ho introduces his friends, **Ling Ling** and **Emily**, to Rachel. Ling Ling is a Chinese student and **Emily** is a Canadian student who are studying with Yoon-ho at the same college. Rachel is taking a Korean class, and she also meets another Korean exchange student, **Jiyoung**, who helps Rachel with her Korean language study. During the course of their study together, they become good friends.

Main characters: Rachel and Yoon-ho
Video clip

5

Part 1

How to use this book

1   Title and Dialogues

Explore the learning goals of each chapter and then take a quick look at the grammar and expressions you will learn. You also can review activities, cultural notes, and vocabulary expansion.

2   Dialogues

Now, jump into the dialogue by reading it through! Speaker names are indicated in green.

3   Word check-up

Read through the vocabulary before reading the dialogue in order to anticipate the meaning and learn key words. We added the Chinese character of the word only if the word is Sino-Korean. Note the abbreviations: n. (noun), adv. (adverb), v. (verb), and adj. (adjective).

4   Video clips

Did you know that all of the dialogues are video-recorded and available on the textbook website? Listen first, then practice the conversation yourself!

5   Translation

In Part 2, the translation is near the dialogue. In Part 3, translations are found at the end of each chapter. Try to understand the meaning of the dialogue by reading and listening first, then check your understanding by looking at the translation.

6   Exercises

After the Grammar and Expressions, useful exercises help you check whether you can put your knowledge of new grammar and expressions to use.

7   Activities

Each chapter has two different activities, designed to be fun and closely related to the grammar and expressions you have learned in the chapter. Practice activities with your friends, classmates, or by yourself! Please refer to the Glossary at the end of the book for unfamiliar words.

8   Vocabulary expansion

Do you want to learn more vocabulary related to the topic of the chapter? This section allows you to expand your vocabulary with a short dialogue. Find out more about unfamiliar words in the Glossary.

9   Cultural notes

You will find small cultural notes through the textbook. These short descriptions of Korean traditions, history, and life are meant to provide background related to the topics in the chapter.

6

Outline of the book

	Lessons	Learning goals	Grammar and expressions	Activities	Cultural notes	Vocabulary expansion
Part 1	**Preparation** Mastering the Korean Alphabet, *Hangeul*	Learners will learn: • Basic Korean vowels and consonants • Pronunciation rules for fluent reading of words in Korean	• Ten basic vowels • Compound vowels • 14 basic consonants • Double consonants	• Can you type in *Hangeul*?		
Part 2	**Lesson 1** Greetings 인사	Learners will be able to: • Introduce themselves • Ask about people's names and where they are from	• 안녕하세요? • 네(예)/아니요. • 한국 사람이에요? • 이름이 뭐예요? • 저는 윤호예요. • 만나서 반가워요. • 제 친구예요. • 어느 나라 사람이에요? • 레이첼 씨, 링링 씨	• "Are you Michael?" • Introducing classmates	• Korean greetings	• Words for self-introduction

continued

7

Part 1

continued

Lessons	Learning goals	Grammar and expressions	Activities	Cultural notes	Vocabulary expansion
Lesson 2 Meals and foods 식사와 음식	Learners will be able to: • Ask and answer questions about favorite foods • Ask questions using demonstratives • Count items, animals, and people using Native-Korean numbers (1–5)	• 먹다/먹어요. • ~좋아해요? • 이게/저게 뭐예요? • 햄버거가 맛있어요. • 음식도 • 카페테리아에 가요. • 그리고/그럼 • 하나, 둘, 셋, 넷, 다섯	• Introducing favorite foods • Inquiring about the food	• Ordering food in Korean • Hot and spicy rice cake	• Words for ordering food
Lesson 3 School life 학교 생활	Learners will be able to: • **Talk about courses they are currently taking** • Ask about the location of their classes	• 알아요/몰라요. • 빅뱅이요. • 한국어를 잘 하고 싶어요. • 한국어 수업을 들어 보세요. • 듣다/들어요. • 그런데, 그래서 • 수학 수업은 어디에서 해요? • 어때요?, 괜찮아요, 그래요?	• Poster fair • Weekly class schedules	• Universities in Korea • K-pop	• Words for majors at college
Lesson 4 Dating 데이트하기	Learners will be able to: • Ask for the time of day and phone numbers • Ask about the price of certain items	• 시간 있어요? • 몇 시예요? • 게임이 몇 시에 있어요? • 윤호 씨하고 같이 가고 싶어요. • 제 전화번호는 123-4567 이에요. • 지금 어디예요? • 얼마예요?	• My dating plan 1 • My dating plan 2	• Korean currency, "won" • Korea– Yonsei varsity games	• Words for sports

Outline of the book

	Lessons	Learning goals	Grammar and expressions	Activities	Cultural notes	Vocabulary expansion
Part 3	**Lesson 5** Weather and health 날씨와 건강	Learners will learn: • Past-tense forms • Phrases for describing the weather or health	• 흐려요. • 날씨가 참 좋네요. • 공부 많이 했어요? • 안/못 했어요. • 윤호 씨는요? 김 선생님은요? • 목도 아프고 열도 있어요.	• Let's talk about the weather around the world • Writing a letter	• Korean home remedies • How to say "thank you" in Korean	• Words to use in hospitals
	Lesson 6 Thanksgiving Day and Chuseok 추수감사절과 추석	Learners will be able to: • Make inquiries about words/ expressions • Describe things, people, and animals • Make suggestions	• 무슨 음식을 먹어요? • 한국어로 ____ (이/가) 뭐예요? • 불고기하고 떡볶이 • 추석이 언제예요? • 추석에 뭐 했어요? • 반달처럼 생겼어요. • 떡볶이를 만들어서 친구하고 같이 먹었어요. • 윷놀이 게임을 해 볼까요?	• Role play: Thanksgiving Day • Let's play Yut	• When is Chuseok? • On your way home for Chuseok	• Words for holidays
	Lesson 7 Korean markets and college clubs/student organizations 한인 마트와 대학 동아리	Learners will be able to: • Explain a purpose for going places • Use future-tense forms • Describe actions in progress	• 김치를 먹어 보세요. • 같이 갈 수 있어요? • 어떡하지요? • 사진을 찍으러 호수에 갔어요. • 태권도를 배우고 있어요. • 안경을 썼어요. • 처음에는 힘들었는데 . . . • 물어볼게요.	• Visiting local Korean markets • My social network	• Korean Street Foods • Korean markets in the United States • College clubs and organizations	• Words for college clubs

continued

9

Part 1

continued

Lessons	Learning goals	Grammar and expressions	Activities	Cultural notes	Vocabulary expansion
Lesson 8 Studying Korean 한국어 공부하기	Learners will be able to: • Express reasons for actions • Make stronger suggestions • Use simple conditional clauses	• 한국어가 재미있어서 . . . • 열심히 하려고 해요. • 대화를 많이 들으면 . . . • 연습하세요/ 연습하지 마세요. • 저는 한국에서 온 교환학생이에요. • 한국 문화에 대해서 . . . • 저도요.	• Ways of studying Korean • Interviewing your friends	• Korean language programs in Korea • What do you like to do with your Korean friends?	• Words for study skills

Preparation

Mastering the Korean alphabet, *Hangeul*

Do you know how many vowels and consonants there are in the Korean alphabet? The Korean alphabet has 24 basic letters (i.e., ten basic vowels and 14 basic consonants). The Korean alphabet is often called *Hangeul*, but the meaning of *Hangeul* can be extended further as "the Korean writing system" or "Korean writings in general." Here, in this textbook, we refer to the Korean alphabet as *Hangeul*. Before we talk in detail, about the **Korean alphabet,** you might wonder about the vowels and consonants, and how they are defined in the first place. According to the Merriam-Webster dictionary, a **vowel** is a speech sound that is made with your mouth open and your tongue in the middle of your mouth, not touching your teeth, lips, etc. The English letters *a, e, i, o, u,* and (sometimes) *y* represent vowels. **A consonant** is defined as "a speech sound that is made by partially or completely stopping the flow of air breathed from the mouth," and any letters except *a, e, i, o, u,* and (sometimes) *y* represent consonants. Given this, the Korean alphabet is defined as the written representation of Korean speech sounds (vowels, consonants) and its combinations. Next, we will discuss the following:

- A quick history of *Hangeul*
- Vowels and consonants in *Hangeul*
- Ten basic Korean vowels
- 14 basic Korean consonants
- Combinations of vowels with consonants: Vertical or horizontal vowels
- Compound vowels in Korean
- Double consonants in Korean
- Syllable-final consonants in Korean
- Pronunciation of syllable-final consonants
- Pronunciation of compound consonants in syllable-final position
- Fluent reading of words and sentences in Korean

Part 1

A quick history of *Hangeul*

The Korean alphabet, *Hangeul*, was created in 1443 during the Chosun Dynasty by the fourth monarch King Sejong (세종대왕) and his scholars at *Jiphyeonjeon* (집현전), a royal institution. Society in the Chosun Dynasty was governed strictly based on classes. While upper-class people knew and used Chinese characters for reading and writing, lower-class people didn't know how to read and write in Chinese characters because they didn't have any educational opportunities to learn them. King Sejong was deeply concerned about the situation since this meant that his own people (especially the lower class) could not read, write or keep any records in written form. Thus, along with his scholars, he dedicated himself to the creation of a new writing system that would allow anyone, regardless of class, to read and write on their own. King Sejong came up with the ways in which Korean consonants and vowels are arranged into syllabic blocks by observing the grids in traditional Korean windows. The shapes of some basic Korean letters were designed to resemble the shapes of the mouth, lips, and vocal folds.

King Sejong traditional Korean window
Source: Pixabay.com

Let's take a closer look at the following Korean syllables. Discuss their shapes with your classmates. (A **syllable** is a unit of pronunciation having one vowel sound, with or without surrounding consonants, forming the whole or a part of word. For example, "water" has two syllables and "inferno" has three syllables.)

1   What images come to your mind when you look at the shapes?
2   Do you have any ideas and thoughts about the shapes?
3   Do you find any interesting shapes?

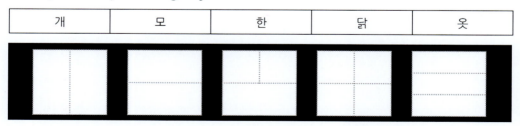

Diverse combination of consonants and vowels

Preparation

In the figure, the dotted lines indicate areas in which each consonant or vowel is situated. For example, the first syllable (개) shows two areas: one for the consonant ㄱ and another for the vowel ㅐ, and both are combined within a virtual syllabic block. The second syllable (모) has the consonant ㅁ on top and the vowel ㅗ placed below. The third syllable (한) shows three separate areas within the syllabic block: Beginning with the consonant ㅎ, the vowel ㅏ is added, and then the consonant ㄴ is placed below them both. The fourth syllable (닭) has four areas within the syllabic block: Beginning at the top left, the consonant ㄷ is combined with the vowel ㅏ, then the two consonants ㄹ and ㄱ are arranged in a row beneath them. Finally, the last syllable (옷) has three horizontal areas: The empty filler consonant ㅇ is placed on top, with the vowel ㅗ in the middle, and finally the consonant ㅅ.

Vowels and consonants in *Hangeul*

Basically, Korean vowels and consonants are composed of lines and dots. As shown in the following figure, Korean vowels and consonants are the combinations of lines and dots in varying degrees of the orientation of lines (e.g., vertical or horizontal), or the location of the dots in relation to the lines (e.g., top, bottom, left or right).

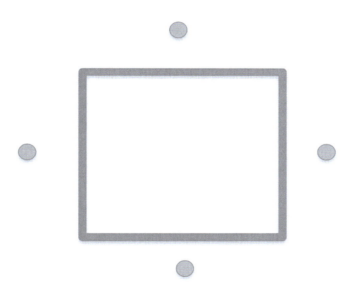

Elements of Korean alphabet: Dots and lines

In Confucianism, dots mean "sky," horizontal lines mean "earth" and vertical lines mean "humans" – and these three components (i.e., sky, earth, and humans) represent the universe. With these three elements in mind, the Korean Alphabet was created with the aim and ambition that it can describe all of the aspects of the universe using the *Hangeul* writing system. Here are specific examples of how lines and dots are combined to create vowels and consonants in Korean.

13

Part 1

(1) Korean vowels ㅏ and ㅗ   (2) Korean consonants ㄱ and ㅋ

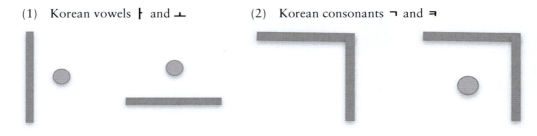

As shown in (1), a long vertical line followed by a dot was designed for the basic Korean vowel ㅏ pronounced [ah] while a dot on top with a long horizontal line underneath it is another basic Korean vowel ㅗ pronounced [oh]. The combination of the line and dot is also found in the Korean consonants as shown in (2). A horizontal line connected with vertical line represents a basic Korean consonant ㄱ, which is pronounced similar to [g]. If you add an additional dot to this basic consonant, you create another Korean consonant: ㅋ, which is pronounced [k]. In the following sections, let's talk more about Korean vowels and consonants.

Ten basic Korean vowels

We will begin with the ten basic vowels in Korean.

	Ten basic vowels					
(1)	ㅏ [ah]	ㅓ [eo]	ㅗ [o]	ㅜ [u]	ㅡ [eu]	ㅣ [i]
(2)	ㅑ [yah]	ㅕ [yeo]	ㅛ [yo]	ㅠ [yu]		

Of those ten basic vowels, (1) includes the forms and pronunciations of the most basic vowels in Korean. Each language has different speech sounds that might sound similar to the speech sounds in other languages. It can be quite challenging to perceive certain speech sounds of a new language based on native languages of yours. Rather, we probably approximate speech sounds using other languages. Here, we are trying to give you a sense of how the Korean basic vowels sound by using English words:

  ㅏ → father, ahh
  ㅓ → cup, uh-oh
  ㅗ → oh, poke
  ㅜ → oops, boot, mood
  ㅡ → no matching English sound (or maybe "e" as in "taken")
  ㅣ → keep, feet, key

Given this, if you add another short line or stroke to the first four basic vowels, you can have the vowels in (2) with similar speech sounds in English as shown:

  ㅑ → yahoo, yarn, yard
  ㅕ → young, onion
  ㅛ → yo, yoke, yoga
  ㅠ → you, youth, Yule

By now, you've probably figured out that adding an extra line to the basic vowels means to the addition of "y" – sound to each vowel. Let's practice again with the basic vowels first, and then with y added to the vowels.

[Practice]

Let's repeat the following sets of the vowels.

1 ㅏ, ㅓ, ㅗ, ㅜ → ㅑ, ㅕ, ㅛ, ㅠ
2 ㅑ, ㅕ, ㅛ, ㅠ → ㅏ, ㅓ, ㅗ, ─
3 ㅏ, ㅑ, ㅓ, ㅕ, ㅗ, ㅛ, ㅜ, ㅠ, ─, ㅣ

14 Basic Korean consonants

Let's learn more about the basic Korean consonants.

14 basic consonants								
(1)	ㄱ [g/k]	ㄴ [n]	ㄷ [d/t]	ㄹ [r/l]	ㅁ [m]	ㅂ [b/p]	ㅅ [s]	ㅇ no sound
(2)							ㅈ [j/dz]	
(3)	ㅋ [k]		ㅌ [t]			ㅍ [p]	ㅊ [ch]	ㅎ [h]

Here are equivalent sounds from English words for the Korean consonants:

ㄱ → go, get,
ㄴ → name, no
ㄷ → do/tow, doll/toll
ㄹ → red, lamp
ㅁ → man, milk
ㅂ → boy/park
ㅅ → soul, sleep
ㅇ → no sound value (syllable-finally, this symbol sounds like [ng])
ㅈ → joy, joke,
ㅊ → chill, chair, church
ㅋ → kind, kill
ㅌ → talk, tea, tide
ㅍ → pie, peak
ㅎ → hope, hat

As mentioned, it is quite challenging (almost impossible) to describe some Korean consonants by using English consonents. For example, the consonant ㄱ may sound like a speech sound similar to the English [g] and [k]. Depending on your native language, the Korean consonant ㄱ may sound closer to [g]. To others, it may sound closer to [k].

15

Part 1

Combinations of vowels with consonants: vertical or horizontal vowels

We have just learned ten vowels and 14 consonants in Korean, and we will now talk about the ways in which these are combined. In principle, there are certain ways in which vowels and consonants are combined:

1. Korean vowels and consonants are arranged fitting into (virtual) syllabic blocks.
2. Each syllable begins with a consonant.
3. Consonants and vowels are combined from left to right or top to bottom.

Here are examples of the consonant ㄱ combined with various vowels:

가   거   고   구   그   기

Regarding the orientation of the vowels in relation to the consonant ㄱ, the vowels are placed either vertically or horizontally as shown in the following figure: (C: consonant; V: vowel)

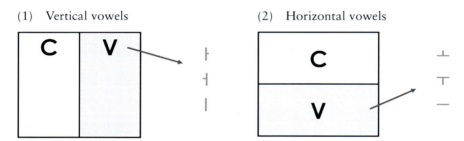

Learning the pronunciation of the vowels and consonants

To develop a pronunciation similar to a native speaker of Korean, do not rely on speech sounds found in English words for Korean vowels and consonants. As mentioned, they are just equivalent sounds from English. Rather, practice repeating what the native speakers (e.g., your instructors, Korean friends etc.) pronounce for you. For example, if you have a Korean friend or tutor, ask him/her to read the vowels and consonants for you. Then, repeat them by imitating their pronunciation as closely as possible until you feel comfortable to read the Korean vowel and consonant letters by yourself.

[Practice 1]

Here is a chart to help you practice combining all of the consonants and vowels. While combining of the consonants and vowels, also pronounce each combination.

	ㅏ	ㅑ	ㅓ	ㅕ	ㅗ	ㅛ	ㅜ	ㅠ	ㅡ	ㅣ
ㄱ	가	야	거	겨	고	교	구	규	그	기
ㄴ		냐								니

ㄷ			더						드	
ㄹ				려				류		
ㅁ					모		무			
ㅂ						뵤				
ㅅ					소		수			
ㅇ				여				유		
ㅈ			저						즈	
ㅊ		차								치
ㅋ	카								크	
ㅌ								튜		
ㅍ							푸			
ㅎ						효				

[Practice 2]

Read aloud the following combination of consonants and vowels:

1 가 – 나 – 다 – 라 – 마 – 바 – 사 – 아 – 자 – 차 – 카 – 타 – 파 – 하
2 고 – 노 – 도 – 로 – 모 – 보 – 소 – 오 – 조 – 초 – 코 – 토 – 포 – 호
3 아 – 야 – 어 – 여 – 오 – 요 – 우 – 유 – 으 – 이
4 마 – 먀 – 머 – 며 – 모 – 묘 – 무 – 뮤 – 므 – 미

Compound vowels in Korean

In this section, we will learn about compound vowels in Korean. More than one vowel are combined together to create new vowels. In principle, additional vowels (i.e., ㅣ, ㅏ, ㅓ) are added to the basic ten vowels as shown here.

	Ten basic vowels									
	ㅏ	ㅑ	ㅓ	ㅕ	ㅗ	ㅛ	ㅜ	ㅠ	ㅡ	ㅣ
(1)	ㅐ [ae]	ㅒ [yae]	ㅔ [e]	ㅖ [ye]	ㅚ [oe]		ㅟ [wi]		ㅢ [ui]	
(2)					ㅘ [wa]					
(3)							ㅝ [wo]			
(4)					ㅙ [wae]		ㅞ [we]			

Part 1

The vowels in row (1) show the combination of the basic vowels with the vowel ㅣ. For example, the vowel ㅐ is equivalent to the combination of the vowels ㅏ plus ㅣ. In moving further, an additional line or stroke is added to this ㅐ, and this ㅣ + ㅐ combination creates ㅒ and it is pronounced [yae]. In a similar way, the vowel ㅓ is combined with ㅣ, resulting in ㅔ pronounced [e]. Add an additional ㅣ to ㅔ, we have ㅖ pronounced [ye] like English "yea."

Adding ㅣ (i.e., y-like sound) to vowels:

- ㅣ + ㅐ → ㅒ
- ㅣ + ㅔ → ㅖ

The remaining vowels in (1) ㅚ, ㅟ, ㅢ are interesting in that they end with the vowel ㅣ as shown:

- ㅗ + ㅣ → ㅚ: start with ㅗ [o] and finish with ㅣ [i]
- ㅜ + ㅣ → ㅟ: start with ㅜ [u] and finish with ㅣ [i]
- ㅡ + ㅣ → ㅢ: start with ㅡ [eu] and finish with ㅣ [i]

The vowel in row (2) in the table above indicates the addition of the vowel ㅏ to the vowel ㅗ resulting in ㅘ pronounced [wa]. In a similar way, the vowel ㅓ is combined to the vowel ㅜ (i.e., ㅜ + ㅓ → ㅝ) and pronounced [wo] as shown in (3).

Finally, the vowels in row (4) show multiple combinations of the vowels: for ㅙ, ㅗ + ㅏ + ㅣ; for ㅞ, ㅜ + ㅓ + ㅣ.

[Practice]

Read aloud the following syllables and words.

1   과 – 괘 – 괴 – 귀 – 궤 – 궈
2   나눠 – 나녀 – 나뉘 – 나누 – 나노
3   시계 – 가게 – 위 – 귀 – 와이 – 왜
4   의사 – 의자 – 의아 – 사과 – 사귀 – 돼지 – 가위 – 외가 – 과자
5   웨하스 – 하우스 – 뉴 웨이브 – 슈퍼 – 워너비 – 위너 – 웨이터 – 와이프 – 키위

Double consonants in Korean

Previously, we introduced 14 basic Korean consonants. In this section, we will introduce five additional consonants. These five consonants are made by doubling the basic consonants, as shown in (2):

Basic consonants					
(1)	ㄱ	ㄷ	ㅂ	ㅅ	ㅈ
(2)	ㄲ	ㄸ	ㅃ	ㅆ	ㅉ
(3)	ㅋ	ㅌ	ㅍ		ㅊ

18

As for the pronunciation of the double consonants, it is hard to find equivalent sounds in English. Probably somewhat similar sounds would be the pronunciation of stops after "s" within these consonant clusters in English:

ㄲ → "k" as in sky, ski
ㄸ → "t" as in stool, study
ㅃ → "p" as in spam, spy
ㅆ → "s" seal, soul
ㅉ → no equivalent sound in English

The double consonants in row (2) are also called **tensed** consonants because when they are pronounced, you can feel tension in the vocal folds (or along the Adam's apple area). But do not worry about this terminology. Rather, listen to your Korean instructors or friend's pronunciation of these, and try to imitate their pronunciation. We previously encountered the consonants in row (3). When you pronounce these consonants, you feel more air puffing from the mouth.

Pronounce the following words with a piece of paper in front of your mouth.

카	타	파	하

You will notice some air puffing out of your mouth when you pronounce these Korean syllables. For that reason, these consonants are also called **aspirated** consonants. You will soon realize how challenging it is to differentiate these three groups of consonants in perceiving and pronouncing them. Here are some examples of real Korean words:

1 굴 꿀 쿨
2 달 딸 탈
3 불 뿔 풀
4 살 쌀
5 자다 짜다 차다

[Practice 1]

Read the following words aloud to yourself.

1 까마귀 뽀뽀 토끼 도끼
2 오빠 오바 오버 오퍼
3 뿌리 부리 푸리 보리
4 아저씨 아가씨 아빠
5 가마 카마 까마

[Practice 2]

Read to your classmates one word from the choice of three words each, then, ask them to point out which ones you pronounced.

1 개다 캐다 깨다
2 그 크 끄
3 지우다 치우다 찌우다
4 비 피 삐
5 사다 싸다 자다

Part 1

Syllable-final consonants in Korean

In this section, we will focus on the Korean consonants in **syllable-final** position. By syllable-final, we mean the "t" in ca**t**, the "p" in co**p**, for example. In Korean we have two possible situations in relation to the orientation of the vowels, as shown here:

(1) Syllable-final consonants with vertical vowels

(2) Syllable-final consonants with horizontal vowels

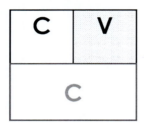
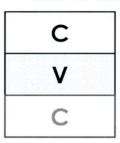

While 19 Korean consonants (i.e., 14 basic consonants and five double consonants) can appear in syllable-initial position (e.g., **c**at/Bo**b**), there are a limited number of consonants (and pronunciations) allowed in syllable-final position. This means some syllable-initial consonants will go through a so-called syllable-final **simplification** or **neutralization** process in terms of pronunciation.

Pronunciation of syllable-final consonants

Regarding the pronunciation of syllable-final consonants, in this section we will show how some consonants in the syllable-final position are simplified or neutralized when they appear in syllable-initial position.

1 Pronunciation of ㄴ, ㅁ in syllable-final position:

Syllable-initial position	Syllable-final position
• ㄴ [n] → 나 [na] • ㅁ [m] → 마 [ma]	• ㄴ [n] → 간 [gan] • ㅁ [m] → 감 [gam]

2 Pronunciation of ㄹ, ㅇ in syllable-final position:

Syllable-initial position	Syllable-final position
• ㄹ [r] → 라 [ra] • ㅇ [no sound value] → 아	• ㄹ [l] → 갈 [gal] • ㅇ [ng] → 강 [gang]

3 Pronunciation of ㄱ, ㅋ, ㄲ in syllable-final position:

Syllable-initial position	Syllable-final position
• ㄱ [g] → 가 [ga] • ㅋ [k] → 카 [ka] • ㄲ [kk] → 까 [kka]	• ㄱ [k] → 악 [ak] neutralized • ㅋ [k] → 악 [ak] neutralized • ㄲ [k] → 악 [ak] neutralized

Preparation

4   Pronunciation of ㅂ, ㅍ, ㅃ in syllable-final position:

Syllable-initial position	Syllable-final position
• ㅂ [b] → 바 [ba] • ㅍ [p] → 파 [pa] • ㅃ [pp] → 빠 [ppa]	• ㅂ [p] → 압 [ap] neutralized • ㅍ [p] → 앞 [ap] neutralized • ㅃ is not allowed syllable-finally.

5   Pronunciation of ㄷ, ㅌ, ㄸ, ㅅ, ㅆ, ㅈ, ㅉ, ㅊ, ㅎ in syllable-final position:

Syllable-initial position	Syllable-final position
• ㄷ [d/t] → 다 [da] • ㅌ [t] → 타 [ta] • ㄸ [tt] → 따 [tta] • ㅅ [s] → 사 [sa] • ㅆ [ss] → 싸 [ssa] • ㅈ [j] → 자 [ja] • ㅉ [jj] → 짜 [jja] • ㅊ [ch] → 차 [cha] • ㅎ [h] → 하 [ha]	• ㄷ [t] → 앋 [at] neutralized • ㅌ [t] → 앝 [at] neutralized • ㄸ is not allowed syllable-finally. • ㅅ [t] → 앗 [at] neutralized • ㅆ [t] → 았 [at] neutralized • ㅈ [t] → 앚 [at] neutralized • ㅉ is not allowed syllable-finally. • ㅊ [t] → 앛 [at] neutralized • ㅎ [t] → 앟 [at] neutralized

By now you may be overwhelmed by the simplification/neutralization process in syllable-final position. It is surely not an easy task to study this phenomenon. Just hang in there. Here is a summary chart for you:

	Syllable-final position						
Pronunciation	ㄱ [k]	ㄴ [n]	ㄷ [t]	ㄹ [l]	ㅁ [m]	ㅂ [p]	ㅇ [ng]
Letters of syllable-final consonants	ㄱ, ㅋ, ㄲ	ㄴ	ㄷ, ㅌ, ㅅ, ㅆ, ㅈ, ㅊ, ㅎ	ㄹ	ㅁ	ㅂ, ㅍ	ㅇ

[Practice 1]

Read the following syllables out loud.

1	앋	곧	눋	벋	싣
2	압	곱	눕	법	십
3	앙	공	눙	벙	싱
4	알	골	눌	벌	실
5	암	곰	눔	범	심
6	안	곤	눈	번	신
7	악	곡	눅	벅	식

21

Part 1

[Practice 2]

Read the following words out loud.

1 고향 고양이 옹알이 항아리 웅덩이
2 밤 알밤 밤꽃 벚꽃 벌꽃
3 갈비 갈치 가을 노을 꽃길
4 한강 남강 갈망 소망 희망
5 악독 극악 쇄약 허락 부엌

Pronunciation of compound consonants in syllable-final position

In this section we will learn how to read Korean syllables ending with more than one consonant. Here are some examples of Korean words with compound consonants in the syllable-final position:

1 ㄱㅅ: 넋 (soul, spirit), 몫 (portion)
2 ㄹㄱ: 닭 (chicken), 읽다 (to read)
3 ㅂㅅ: 없다 (not to have), 값 (price)
4 ㄴㅈ: 앉다 (to sit), 얹다 (to put/place)
5 ㄴㅎ: 않다 (not to do), 많다 (to be many/much)
6 ㄹㅂ: 넓다 (to be spacious), 짧다 (to be short)
7 ㄹㅅ: 돐 (one-year anniversary)
8 ㄹㅌ: 핥다 (to lick), 훑다 (to scan, search for)
9 ㄹㅍ: 읊다 (to recite)
10 ㄹㅁ: 삶 (life), 굶다 (to skip meals), 젊다 (to be young)

How do we read these compound consonants? Here is how we do it:

	Syllable-final position									
Pronunciation	ㄱ [k]	ㄱ [k]	ㅂ [p]	ㄴ [n]	ㄴ [n]	ㄹ [l]	ㄹ [l]	ㄹ [l]	ㄹ [l]	ㅁ [m]
Compound consonants	ㄱㅅ	ㄹㄱ	ㅂㅅ	ㄴㅈ	ㄴㅎ	ㄹㅂ	ㄹㅅ	ㄹㅌ	ㄹㅍ	ㄹㅁ

Go back to the word lists in (1) through (8), and read them again. Of those compound consonants in syllable-final position, you choose one consonant for pronunciation as follows:

1 넋 → [넉], 몫 → [목]
2 닭 → [닥], 읽다 → [익 –]
3 없다 → [업 –], 값 → [갑]
4 앉다 → [안 –], 얹다 → [언 –]
5 않다 → [안 –], 많다 → [만 –]
6 넓다 → [널 –], 짧다 → [짤-]
7 돐 → [돌]
8 핥다 → [할-], 훑다 → [홀 –]

22

9 읊다 → [을 –]
10 삶 → [삼], 굶다 → [굼 –], 젊다 → [점 –]

Are there any rules for the pronunciation of these compound consonants?

Except for the compound consonant ㄹㄱ (e.g., 닭, 읽다) it seems that a more sonorous consonant is chosen (e.g., for example, of those ㄴㅈ, ㄴㅎ, ㄴ is more sonorous than the other consonants) for the pronunciation of these compound consonants in the syllable-final position.

Fluent reading of words and sentences in Korean

We have learned thus far a total of 40 vowels and consonants in Korean (21 vowels and 19 consonants) as shown in the following table.

40 vowels and consonants in Korean	
(1) Ten basic vowels	ㅏ, ㅑ, ㅓ, ㅕ, ㅗ, ㅛ, ㅜ, ㅠ, ㅡ, ㅣ
(2) 11 compound vowels	ㅐ, ㅒ, ㅔ, ㅖ, ㅘ, ㅙ, ㅚ, ㅝ, ㅞ, ㅟ, ㅢ
(3) 14 basic consonants	ㄱ, ㄴ, ㄷ, ㄹ, ㅁ, ㅂ, ㅅ, ㅇ, ㅈ, ㅊ, ㅋ, ㅌ, ㅍ, ㅎ
(4) Five double consonants	ㄲ, ㄸ, ㅃ, ㅆ, ㅉ

Combining these vowels and consonants creates indefinite numbers of words. We are now ready to read any words and sentences written with the Korean Alphabet even though we may not yet fully understand what these words or sentences mean.

In this section, we will talk about important pronunciation rules for fluent reading of words and sentences in Korean.

1 **Linking** or **re-syllabification rule**: When a syllable-final consonant is followed by another vowel of the following syllable, the consonant is carried over to the next syllable. Here are some examples of this rule:
   - 단어 → [다너]: The first syllable ends with a consonant (ㄴ), which is followed by another vowel (ㅓ). In this environment, the final consonant (ㄴ) is linked to the following vowel (ㅓ) and thus is pronounced [다.너].
   - 읽어요 → [일거요]: The first syllable ends with two consonants (ㄹㄱ) and a vowel follows. Thus, the last consonant (ㄱ) is carried over to the second syllable. The three-syllable word 읽어요 is pronounced [일.거.요].

   Here are more examples:
   - 음악 → [으막]
   - 먹으니 → [머그니]
   - 있어요 → [이써요]
   - 찾아요 → [차자요]
   - 꽃이 → [꼬치]

Part 1

2 **Nasal assimilation rule**: When a syllable-final stop consonant such as ㅂ [p], ㄷ [t], or ㄱ [k] is followed by a nasal such as ㄴ [n], or ㅁ [m], the stop consonant is assimilated to the following nasal.
- 갑니다 → [감니다]
- 앞문 → [암문]
- 국민 → [궁민]
- 몇년 → [면년]

You may be confused about which stop consonants turn into (or assimilated into) which nasal. Here is a summary chart:

Syllable-final consonants	When followed by a nasal	Assimilated into nasals
ㄱ, ㅋ, ㄲ	ㄴ [n]	→ ㅇ [ng]
ㄷ, ㅆ, ㅊ, ㅌ, ㅎ	ㅁ [m]	→ ㄴ [n]
ㅂ, ㅍ		→ ㅁ [m]

3 **Aspiration rule**: When consonants the ㄱ, ㄷ, ㅂ, ㅈ come before or after ㅎ, the consonants become aspirated, resulting in ㅋ, ㅌ, ㅍ, ㅊ (i.e., ㄱ → ㅋ; ㄷ → ㅌ; ㅂ → ㅍ; ㅈ → ㅊ).
- 어떻게 → [어떠케]: ㅎ + ㄱ → ㅋ
- 좋다 → [조타]: ㅎ + ㄷ → ㅌ
- 많다 → [만타]: ㅎ + ㄷ → ㅌ
- 좋지요 → [조치요]: ㅎ + ㅈ → ㅊ
- 축하 → [추카]: ㄱ + ㅎ → ㅋ
- 특히 → [트키]: ㄱ + ㅎ → ㅋ
- 입학 → [이팍]: ㅂ + ㅎ → ㅍ

24

Activity

Can you type in *Hangeul*?

Using either your phone or computer, let's type the following Korean sentences.

1. 안녕하세요? Hello!
2. 오늘 학교에 가요. I am going to school.
3. 한글을 배워요. I am studying *Hangeul* the Korean alphabet.

If you are not familiar with typing in Korean, here is the Korean keyboard layout for your practice.

Korean typing keyboard to type Korean sentences

How do you type double consonants (e. g., ㅃ, ㅉ, ㄸ, ㄲ, ㅆ) or compound vowels (e. g., ㅐ, ㅔ)? Use the Shift keys.

Part 2

Contents
1. Greetings 인사
2. Meals and foods 식사와 음식
3. School life 학교 생활
4. Dating 데이트하기

Lesson 1

Greetings 인사

Learning goals

- Introduce yourself.
- Ask about people's names and where they are from.

Grammar and expressions

- 안녕하세요? Say "Hello" in Korean.
- 네(예)/아니요. How do we say "Yes" and "No" in Korean?
- 한국 사람이에요? Questions in Korean
- 이름이 뭐예요? What is your name?
- 저는 윤호예요. I am Yoon-ho.
- 만나서 반가워요. Nice to meet you.
- 제 친구예요. This is my friend.
- 어느 나라 사람이에요? What country are you from? (= Where are you from?)
- 레이첼 씨, 링링 씨 What is this '씨' for?

Activities

- "Are you Michael?"
- Introducing classmates

Part 2

Video clip

Cultural notes
- Korean greetings

Vocabulary expansion
- Words for self-introduction

Lesson 1: Greetings 인사

DIALOGUE 1

Hello? 안녕하세요?

At the new student orientation, Rachel, an American college student, meets Yoon-ho, an exchange student from Korea.

레이첼: 안녕하세요?

윤호: 안녕하세요?

레이첼: 저 . . . 한국 사람이에요?

윤호: 네, 한국 사람이에요. 미국 사람이에요?

레이첼: 네, 미국 사람이에요.

윤호: 이름이 뭐예요?

레이첼: 저는 레이첼이에요. 이름이 뭐예요?

윤호: 저는 윤호예요.

레이첼: 만나서 반가워요.

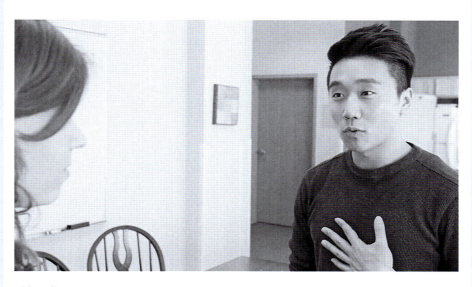

Video clip

Part 2

Word check-up

안녕하세요		Hello, hi
한국 韓國	(n.)	Korea
미국 美國	(n.)	America
한국 사람 韓國人	(n.)	Korean
미국 사람 美國人	(n.)	American
이름	(n.)	name
저 . . .	(adv.)	well . . .
저(는)		honorific form of I (first person)
만나서 (만나다)	(v.)	to meet
반가워요 (반갑다)	(adj.)	to be glad

Rachel: Hello.
Yoon-ho: Hello.
Rachel: Well . . . are you Korean?
Yoon-ho: Yes, I am. Are you American?
Rachel: Yes, I am.
Yoon-ho: What is your name?
Rachel: I am Rachel. What's yours?
Yoon-ho: I am Yoon-ho.
Rachel: Nice to meet you.

DIALOGUE 2

I'm American. 저는 미국 사람이에요

Yoon-ho introduces his friends, Ling Ling and Emily, to Rachel.

윤호: 레이첼 씨, 제 친구예요.
레이첼: 안녕하세요? 저는 레이첼이에요.
링링: 안녕하세요? 저는 링링이에요.
에밀리: 안녕하세요? 저는 에밀리예요.
레이첼: 어느 나라 사람이에요?
링링: 저는 중국 사람이에요.
에밀리: 저는 캐나다 사람이에요. 레이첼 씨는 어느 나라 사람이에요?
레이첼: 저는 미국 사람이에요.

Video clip

Part 2

Word check-up

친구 親舊	(n.)	friend(s)
어느		Which
나라	(n.)	country
중국 中國	(n.)	China
캐나다	(n.)	Canada
제		my (possessive)
~씨		title equivalent to Miss, Mr., Ms., or Mrs.

Yoon-ho:	Rachel, these are my friends.
Rachel:	Hello. I'm Rachel.
Ling Ling:	Hello. I'm Ling Ling.
Emily:	Hi. I'm Emily.
Rachel:	Where are you from?
Ling Ling:	I am from China.
Emily:	I am from Canada. Where are you from, Rachel?
Rachel:	I am from the United States.

Grammar and expressions

1 안녕하세요? Say hello in Korean.

The expression **안녕하세요** is a general greeting in Korean that you can use for a variety of situations. For example, you can use it if you want to initiate a conversation with a stranger on the street, subway, etc. or if you want to say hi to your professor or your classmates in the classroom. Here is an example conversation between Michael and his Korean language professor.

[Example]

마이클: **안녕하세요**, 김 선생님? Hello, Professor Kim.
김 선생님: **안녕하세요**, 마이클 씨? Hello, Michael.

As shown in the example, when a person says hi to you with the greeting 안녕하세요?, you greet her/him back by repeating the same greeting 안녕하세요? You use this greeting 안녕하세요? when you want to say hello to the other person(s) or draw their attention regardless of the time you meet with them (e.g., in the morning, in the afternoon, or at night). For instance, you greet your classmates in the morning with 안녕하세요?, and if you meet the same classmates later that day, you can still greet them with 안녕하세요? You may also hear some similar greetings such as 안녕하십니까? or just 안녕? when watching your favorite K-drama or from your Korean friends. As we will talk about these various forms later in this textbook series – let us just focus on the greeting 안녕하세요? for now.

Is 안녕하세요 a question? How do we respond?

As mentioned earlier, the general greeting 안녕하세요 is equivalent to "Hi," "Hello," or "How are you?" in English. When you greet your classmate, Tom, in the morning using 안녕하세요?, for example, he would probably respond with 안녕하세요? This is the same as

34

Lesson 1: Greetings 인사

if you'd greet each other in the morning with "Hi" or "How are you?" in English. As for the specific intonation patterns for questions in Korean, we will soon talk about them in the following section. So now let's practice saying "Hi" or "How are you?" in Korean to your classmates or friends one more time.

[Practice]

Let's say 안녕하세요? to your classmates.

2 네(예)/아니요. How do we say yes and no in Korean?

In Korean, 네 or 예 means yes while 아니요 indicates no. The choice between 네 and 예 is idiosyncratic (meaning that it is up to the person), and there is no difference in meaning between the two. Interestingly, in English "yeah" or "yeh" are informal representation of yes while "nah" is informally used for no:

yes in Korean	no in Korean
네 or 예	아니요

3 한국 사람이에요? Questions in Korean

In English, depending on the type of question, you may have to invert the word order (for yes–no question) or add the helping verb "do" (for wh-questions), as shown here.

● **Yes–no question:** You are Michael. → Are you Michael? (re-arranging word order)
● **Wh-question:** You study Korean. → Do you study Korean? (adding "do" verb in front)

In Korean, you can create a question by simply using rising intonation at the end of the sentence, as shown here.

- Statement: 한국 사람이에요.

- Question: 한국 사람이에요?

1 한국 사람이에요. You are Korean. (Statement: **Falling intonation** at the end of the sentence)

2 한국 사람이에요? Are you Korean? (Question: **Rising intonation** at the end of the sentence)

As you learn more about Korean, you may also encounter things called "question markers" (e.g., the 안녕하십니까? 한국사람입니까?, '~까?' question marker). As we will gradually introduce those throughout the textbook series, let us now focus on the speech style that you will hear commonly from your Korean friends. Here is a sample conversation between and Michael and Professor Kim in which they exchange questions and answers in Korean.

[Example]

마이클:　　　김 선생님, 한국 사람이에요? Professor Kim, are you Korean?
김 선생님:　네, 한국 사람이에요. Yes, I am Korean.
　　　　　　마이클 씨, 한국 사람이에요? Michael, are you Korean?
마이클:　　　아니요. 저는 미국 사람이에요. No, I am American.

35

Part 2

Double-check

How do we say "Yes" and "No" in Korean?

If you are Korean: 한국 사람이에요? → 네 (or 예), 저는 한국 사람이에요.
If you are American: 한국 사람이에요? → **아니요**. 저는 미국 사람이에요.

4 이름이 뭐예요? What is your name?

On campus you just met someone, and you want to know his/her name: Here is how you ask the question in Korean:

이름이 뭐예요? What is your name?
Okay, repeat this question again: **이름이 뭐예요?**

Here is a scene where Michael asks for Yoon-ho's name. In return, Yoon-ho also asks the same question of Michael.

[Example]

마이클: 이름이 뭐예요? What is your name?
윤호: 저는 윤호예요. 이름이 뭐예요? I am Yoon-ho. What is your name?
마이클: 저는 마이클이에요. I am Michael.

In the following section, we will talk more about the structure 저는 _____ 이에요/예요 for answering the question 이름이 뭐예요? (= What is your name?)

5 저는 윤호예요. I am Yoon-ho.

How would you respond to the question 이름이 뭐예요? (= What is your name?) in Korean?

Question: 이름이 뭐예요? What is your name? → 저는 _____ 이에요/예요.
If you are **Tom**, then → 저는 **탐**이에요.
If you are **Jane**, then → 저는 **제인**이에요.
If you are **Mike**, then → 저는 **마이크**예요.
If you are **Mary**, then → 저는 **매리**예요.
→ 저는 _____ 이에요 or 저는 _____ 예요.
→ I am [your name].

Depending on your name represented in Korean (like 탐 Tom or 마이크 Mike), the structure 저는 _____ 이에요/예요 is used to respond to "What is your name?" in Korean.

At this point, you might wonder what this 저는 _____ 이에요/예요 structure really means in Korean, and when and how you use _____ 이에요 over _____ 예요 in this 저는 _____ 이에요/예요 structure.

~는 (as in 저는) is one of the particles in Korean; it is often called the "topic marker" or "topic particle." A particle shows the relationship of a word or a phrase to the rest of the sentence. More specifically, some particles indicate grammatical functions such as subject, object, or indirect object while other particles carry meanings themselves. If your native language does not include many particles (or markers), you may find this unfamiliar. Unlike English, Korean has numerous particles, which we will introduce one at a time with ample examples throughout the book. So, do not worry! Let's focus on the particle (or marker) 는 in '저는' now:

저는 윤호예요. I am Yoon-ho.
저는 탐이에요. I am Tom.

36

Lesson 1: Greetings 인사

As shown, the first person singular pronoun '저' is followed by the particle '는', and it seems that the whole expression '저는' is the subject of the sentence. (However, you will soon find out the whole part 저는 is not always the subject of the sentence.) Just for now, "저는 _____ 이에요/예요" can be translated as "As for me, my name is _____" or simply, "My name is _____."

What is the difference between _____ 이에요 and _____ 예요? Or: When and how do we use these two in our answers?

If your name ends with a consonant (e.g., Tom and Ann), your name (represented in Korean 탐 and 앤) is followed by ~이에요. If your name ends with a vowel and thus represented as such in Korean (e.g., 미나, 매리), your name is followed by ~예요:

- After a **consonant-ending** name (e.g., 탐, 앤) → Add ~이에요.
- After a **vowel-ending** name (e.g., 미나, 매리) → Add ~예요.

The function of ~이에요/예요 is somewhat similar to the English verb "to be": In English, the verb "to be" (called a copula verb) links the subject of a sentence with a complementary noun or an adjective (e.g., I <u>am</u> a student or I <u>am</u> pretty). Depending on the subject pronoun (e.g., I, you, or she/he), the form of the copula is changed (I am . . ./You are . . ./She/he is . . .). In a somewhat similar way, we add ~이에요 after the consonant-ending name while we add ~예요 after the vowel-ending name. Here is another example.

[Example]

Question: 이름이 뭐예요? What is your name?

    Answer 1: 저는 유나예요. I am Yuna.
    Answer 2: 저는 프랑크예요. I am Frank.
    Answer 3: 저는 지영이에요. I am Jiyoung.
    Answer 4: 저는 동진이에요. I am Dong-jin.

[Practice 1]

Ask your classmate's name with the question 이름이 뭐예요?

You: 이름이 뭐예요?

1 Your classmate 1: _____.
2 Your classmate 2: _____.

[Practice 2]

Fill in the blank with appropriate endings (i.e., 이에요 or 예요?).

1 수지 → 저는 수지 _____.
2 앤디 → 저는 앤디 _____.
3 영철 → 저는 영철 _____.
4 레이첼 → 저는 레이첼 _____.

6 만나서 반가워요. Nice to meet you.

Thus far, we've learned how to exchange greetings as well as how to ask someone's name in Korean given the context where you meet this person for the first time. The expression 만나서

37

Part 2

반가워요 can also be used when you meet a person for the first time, and exchange greetings; it adds the idea of "nice to meet you" in Korean. The following example shows how Michael exchanges greetings with Professor Kim when he met the professor for the first time:

[Example]

마이클: 안녕하세요? 만나서 반가워요. Hello, nice to meet you.
김선생님: 안녕하세요? 만나서 반가워요. Hi, nice to meet you.

Double-Check

We have already learned a few greetings in Korean. As we all say, "practice makes perfect." Let us practice one more time before we move on.

1   How do we say "Hi, hello, or how are you?" in Korean? → 안녕하세요?
2   How do we ask the question "What is your name?" in Korean? → 이름이 뭐예요?
3   How do we respond by saying you name? → 저는 _____ 이에요/예요.

   More specifically:

   if you are Tom → 저는 탐이에요. (the consonant – ending name + **~이에요**)
   If you are Yuna → 저는 유나예요. (the vowel – ending name + **~예요**)

   The variation between ~이에요 and ~예요 comes from the principle of the ease of pronunciation in Korean. That is, this variation makes pronunciation easier.

4   How do we say, "Nice to meet you" in Korean? → 만나서 반가워요.

7   제 친구예요. This is my friend.

In this lesson, Yoon-ho introduces his friends to Rachel using the expression 제 친구예요 (this is my friend). The word 친구 means "a friend" or, depending on the context, it could mean more than one friend, as well. The Korean language is not that strict in differentiating "singularity" from "plurality" in the linguistic forms even if the language has the plural marker 들. As a learner of the language, sometimes you may have to rely on your common sense when you use Korean. Here are some specific examples:

1   Yoon-ho introduces his friend to you: 제 친구예요.
2   Yoon-ho introduces his friends to you: 제 친구예요. (= 제 친구들이에요).

   The word 제 is the possessive form of 저, as shown here.

저 as in "I" am Tom	*제 as in "my" friend*
저는 탐이에요.	제 친구예요.

   The possessive form '제' is placed before the item/person/animal (etc.) indicating that the item/person/animal belongs to me as in "my" belonging. Here are more examples of the possessive form '제' plus nouns:

1   제 가방이에요. (That is) my bag.
2   제 컴퓨터예요. (That is) my computer.
3   제 언니예요. (That is) my older sister.
4   제 형이에요. (That is) my older brother.

38

Lesson 1: Greetings 인사

5   제 고양이예요. (That is) my cat.
6   제 강아지예요. (That is) my puppy.
    → 제 (possessive form "my") + noun (possession) + ~이에요/예요.

[Practice]

Using the possessive form '제' + [noun], say the following items belong to me as in "my" things or belongings.

1   책 (book) →
2   핸드폰 (cell phone) →
3   사전 (dictionary) →

8   어느 나라 사람이에요? What country are you from? (= Where are you from?)

After exchanging greetings, you may want to know where the person is from. Here is the expression in Korean:

"어느 나라 사람이에요?"
Let's repeat it slowly one more time:
"어느 나라 사람이에요?"

At this moment, you might wonder what each part "어느 나라 사람이에요?" means. In order to figure that out, here is each vocabulary word used in the question:

1   어느 → which
2   나라 → country
3   사람 → person, people

Given this, you can figure out that the question "어느 나라 사람이에요?" asks "Which country are you from? There are many ways of learning a new language, and you have your own learning styles, too. We don't emphasize that you should take things apart in order to learn a language. Instead, if you are a beginner in any new language, we would recommend that you take the expression as a whole without overanalyzing every part of the expression. Let's practice the question as a whole, then. Repeat this question: "어느 나라 사람이에요?"

Here is a conversation between Professor Kim and Michael:

Professor Kim: 마이클 씨, 어느 나라 사람이에요?
Michael: 저는 미국 사람이에요. 김 선생님, 어느 나라 사람이에요?
Professor Kim: 저는 한국 사람이에요.

[Practice]

Point one of the following flags to your classmates and ask them the question "어느 나라 사람이에요?" Then the classmates answer using the structure 저는 _____ 사람이에요.

9   레이첼 씨, 링링 씨 What is '씨' for?

In this lesson, Yoon-ho addresses Rachel with '레이첼 씨.' You might wonder what the additional word '씨' means right after Rachel's name in Korean. In learning Korean, you will see the language reflects the degree of the relationships of the interlocutors in its linguistic forms.

39

Part 2

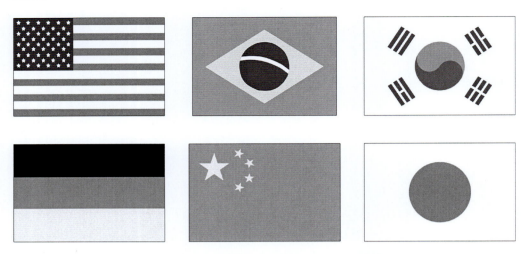

Country flags (the United States, Brazil, South Korea, Germany, China, Japan in order)
Pixabay.com

With sophisticated and developed honorific systems, the Korean language captures hierarchical power dynamics of the ways in which the language is used. Kinship terms (e.g., 어머니, 아버지, 형, 누나, 언니, 동생, 이모) and also job-related professional addressee terms (such as 선생님, 과장님, 사장님, 회장님) are good examples of relation-based and hierarchy-related language use in Korean. In the later part of this textbook, you will be introduced to some of the kinship terms and addressee terms (or titles). Along this line, the word '씨' can be roughly translated as "miss" or "mister" and it is typically used with the first names (as in 레이첼 씨, 윤호 씨, 마이클 씨). Following are examples.

마이클: 지영 씨, 안녕하세요? Hello, Jiyoung!
지영: 아, 마이클 씨. 안녕하세요? Oh, Michael. Hello!

 This conversation shows us that Michael and Jiyoung met before and know (probably slightly) each other, and they sound polite by calling each other with the term '씨'. This indicates they can be classmates, colleagues, or just acquaintances. The term '씨' can also be used with family names as in 김 씨, 박 씨, 최 씨 typically used when the addressees (here 김 씨, 박 씨, 최 씨) are employed and thus provide some kind of service to the other parties. Here is an example of this case.

Boss: 김 씨, 안녕하세요? Hello, Mr. Kim. (Mr. Kim is one of the employees)
Mr. Kim: 사장님, 안녕하세요? Hello, boss!

 As shown in this lesson, Rachel just met Yoon-ho at the orientation and it is likely that they will begin to develop a friendship. That is the context of their relationship at this moment, and, thus, they want to sound polite by calling each other with the term '씨.' Throughout the textbook, we will show you more of relational terms (including kinship terms) along with the explanation of its uses.

Lesson 1: Greetings 인사

Activity 1

"Are you Michael?"

Suppose you are looking for someone named Michael. You do not know if Michael is in this group; therefore, say 마이클이에요? (Are you Michael?) to each person. In response, the group members will answer by saying either 네, 마이클이에요. (Yes, I am Michael) or 아니요, 존이에요. (No, I am John). Let's find "Michael." It is your job!

어느 나라 사람이에요?

Using the deck of country flag cards on your table, ask where your partner is from using the question 어느 나라 사람이에요?

1. Shuffle the cards, then pick one.
2. While holding the card of the US flag, ask John if he is from the United States. He will answer "Yes, I am" in Korean.

You: 미국 사람이에요? Are you an American?
John: 네, 미국 사람이에요. Yes, I am.

3. Ling Ling is Chinese. While holding the US flag, ask her if she is from the United States. She will answer "No, I am not. I am Chinese." in Korean.

You: 미국 사람이에요? Are you an American?
Ling Ling: 아니요. 중국 사람이에요. No, I am not. I am Chinese.

4. Shuffle the cards again and ask each person if they are from any country (you choose the country); they have to answer that they are from the country of the flag they are holding.

Pixabay.com

Part 2

Activity 2

Introducing classmates

On her way home, Linda meets Yoon-ho and his friend. Yoon-ho introduces his friend to Linda. What does he say to Linda? "이름이 뭐예요?" and "어느 나라 사람이에요?"
   Your turn:

1   Make teams of four members.
2   Each team member introduces each other.
3   Each team picks its own team leader.
4   Each team leader then introduces his/her members to the other teams.

Group A

조장 group leader:

조원 이름 names of group members:

이름 your name:

어느 나라 사람이에요?:

Group B

조장:

조원 이름:

이름:

어느 나라 사람이에요?:

Group C

조장:

조원 이름:

이름:

어느 나라 사람이에요?:

Group D

조장:

조원 이름:

이름:

어느 나라 사람이에요?:

Notes for the team leader to introduce team members
Image created by authors

Lesson 1: Greetings 인사

Cultural notes

Korean greetings

In general, the bow is the traditional Korean greeting. It is sometimes accompanied by a handshake. Just like many Asian countries, bowing is both a way to show respect and to say 안녕하세요. Koreans have their own customs related to bowing. A very simple bow to use when meeting someone for the first time, or someone you respect, is to tilt your head downward and say 안녕하세요. If you do this every time you meet a good friend, it looks weird. But when you meet your boss, co-worker, teachers, you may have to show them respect by bowing every time. The deeper you bow the more respect you show. If you are meeting someone casually, you can just tilt your head. Saying 안녕하세요 can be a good start. Bowing is also used when you are thankful.

In Korea, what you say and do to greet people depends on the time of the day, the occasions and the person whom you're greeting. When you're meeting someone for the very first time, you may stretch out your right hand, bowing slightly but not shaking the hands too much, just clasping hands briefly. If you want to show your respect when shaking hands, you can support your right forearm with your left hand. But sometimes you will see some Koreans nod slightly. Younger Korean people wave, moving their arm from side to side. When you initiate the bow, say 안녕하세요, then say 만나서 반가워요, which means "Nice to meet you." When you leave, say 안녕히 계세요 or 안녕히 가세요 (good-bye). Korean people usually say 안녕 when they meet someone and also when they leave – but only to a friend or someone younger than them. When it is time to leave, Korean people have a couple different ways to say good-bye. If you're leaving and the other person is staying, you can say 안녕히 계세요. 계세요 means "Please stay" (literally, "Please stay peacefully"). If the other person is leaving, you can say 안녕히 가세요. 가세요 means "Please go"; 안녕히 가세요 means "Please go peacefully." The more common informal greeting is 안녕, which means "Peace." The more standard greeting that you will hear a lot from Korean people is 안녕하세요, which literally means "Are you at peace?" Korean people use this when they meet someone.

You don't want to hug someone you have just met for the first time. In general, Korean people tend to reserve hugging for couples or for very close friends or family that are saying good-bye for a long time. If you meet future parents-in-law, teachers, a boss, a blind date, or colleagues at an important business meeting, you want to bow low to show great respect. Handshakes may accompany bows, but it is more common for a Korean man to offer a handshake than a woman.

Vocabulary expansion

밑줄 친 단어를 보세요. 상자 안에 있는 단어를 사용해서 다음의 대화를 연습하세요. Please look at the underlined words. Use the words in the box to practice the following conversations.

What do you do?

존: 안녕하세요?
윤호: 안녕하세요?
존: 만나서 반가워요. 저는 **의사** 예요.
윤호: 만나서 반가워요. 저는 **학생** 이에요.
존: 그래요? (Is that right/so?)

43

Part 2

Vocabulary

미술가	artist
사진가	photographer
가수	singer
의사	doctor
간호사	nurse
요리사	chef
농부	farmer
교사	teacher
교수	professor
학생	student
엔지니어	engineer
회사원	businessman

Student
Pixabay.com

Singer
Pixabay.com

Doctor
Pixabay.com

Engineer
Pixabay.com

44

Lesson 2

Meals and foods 식사와 음식

Learning goals

- Ask and answer questions about favorite foods.
- Ask questions using demonstratives.
- Count items, animals, and people using Native-Korean numbers (1–5).

Grammar and expressions

- 먹다/먹어요. Verbal conjugation
- ~좋아해요? Do you like ~?
- 이게/저게 뭐예요? What is this? What is that?
- 햄버거<u>가</u> 맛있어요. Subject particle
- 음식<u>도</u>. Also/too
- 카페테리아<u>에</u> 가요. Destination particle
- 그리고 and/그럼 then
- 하나, 둘, 셋, 넷, 다섯 Counting numbers in Korean: Native-Korean numbers

Activities

- Introducing favorite foods
- Inquiring about the food

45

Part 2

Cultural notes

- Ordering food in Korea
- Hot and spicy rice cake

Vocabulary expansion

- Words for ordering food

Pixabay.com

DIALOGUE 1

I'm hungry. 배고파요

After the new-student orientation is over, Yoon-ho and Rachel are about to have lunch at the school cafeteria.

윤호: 아, 배고파요. 레이첼 씨도 배고파요?
레이첼: 네, 조금 . . . 우리 점심 같이 먹을까요?
윤호: 그래요. 같이 먹어요. 뭐 좋아해요?
레이첼: 음 . . . 햄버거 어때요?
윤호: 햄버거 진짜 좋아해요. 어디 갈까요?
레이첼: 학교 식당에 햄버거가 있어요.
윤호: 그래요? 빨리 가요!

Video clip

Part 2

Word check-up

아	(excl.)	ah
배고파요 (배고프다)	(adj.)	to be hungry
네		yes
~도	(part.)	too/also/as well
조금	(adv.)	some/a little
점심 點心	(n.)	lunch
먹어요 (먹다)	(v.)	to eat
~ㄹ까요?		Shall we ~?
그래요		Yes, okay
그래요?		Is that so?
~어때요?		What about ~?
같이	(adv.)	together
좋아해요 (좋아하다)	(v.)	to like, enjoy
어디(로)	(adv.)	where (to)
햄버거	(n.)	hamburger
진짜	(adv.)	really
학교 學校	(n.)	school
빨리	(adv.)	hurriedly, quickly
~에	(part.)	to ~(place)
가요 (가다)	(v.)	to go

Yoon-ho: Ah, I'm hungry. Are you hungry as well?
Rachel: Yes, a little . . . Shall we eat lunch together?
Yoon-ho: Sure. Let's eat together. What do you like?
Rachel: Umm . . . What about hamburgers?
Yoon-ho: I really like hamburgers. Where do you want to go?
Rachel: There are hamburgers in school cafeteria.
Yoon-ho: Is that so? Let's go! Hurry!

Lesson 2: Meals and foods 식사와 음식

DIALOGUE 2

What's this? 이게 뭐예요?

Rachel and Yoon-ho talk about the menu at the cafeteria.

레이첼: 여기 햄버거가 있어요. 메뉴 보세요.

윤호: 이게 뭐예요?

레이첼: 이게 샌드위치예요.

윤호: 아, 그래요? 그럼 저게 뭐예요?

레이첼: 저게 맥앤치즈예요.

윤호: 맥앤치즈 맛있어요?

레이첼: 아니요, 맛없어요.

윤호: 그럼, 저는 햄버거 주세요. 참, 여기 콜라 있어요?

레이첼: 네, 콜라 있어요. 저도 콜라 주세요.

윤호: 두(2) 잔 주문해요?

레이첼: 네, 좋아요.

49

Part 2

Word check-up

여기	(adv.)	here
있어요 (있다)	(v.)	to be/there is
메뉴	(n.)	menu
보세요 (보다)	(v.)	please look (at)
샌드위치	(n.)	sandwich
이게/저게 뭐예요?		What is this/that?
그럼	(conn.)	then
~주세요		please give me ~
맥앤치즈	(n.)	mac and cheese
맛있어요/맛없어요 (맛있다/맛없다)	(adj.)	to be delicious/not to be delicious
참	(excl.)	by the way
콜라	(n.)	cola
아니요		no
주문해요 (주문하다) 注文 –	(v.)	to order something
~잔 盞	(n.)	counter for cup: e.g., a cup of coffee 커피 한 잔

Rachel: Here, there are hamburgers. Look at the menu.
Yoon-ho: What is this?
Rachel: This is a sandwich.
Yoon-ho: Ah, is that so? Then what is that?
Rachel: That is mac and cheese.
Yoon-ho: Is mac and cheese delicious?
Rachel: No, it is not.
Yoon-ho: Then, I will have a hamburger. By the way, do they have cola?
Rachel: Yes, they have cola. Please give me some cola as well.
Yoon-ho: Shall I order two cups of cola?
Rachel: Sounds good.

Grammar and expressions

1   먹다/먹어요. Verbal conjugation

Learning verbs is tough in any language. If you've studied Spanish or French you've undoubtedly spent a lot of time conjugating verbs. Or, maybe you have heard a learner of English struggle to get the right form of the verb, saying "I goes" or "She go." Verbs are tough in Korean, too. Before we move on, though, let's review the definition of a verb: a word used to describe an action, state, or occurrence. Some common everyday verbs are: wake up, take a shower eat, go (somewhere), study, work, sleep, and write. We'll learn these verbs in Korean, too. Now let's also think about the definition of conjugation: changing the form of the verb. In Korean you don't have to change for person (I,

50

Lesson 2: Meals and foods 식사와 음식

you, she), but you do have to change the verbs in other ways. We will show you how to do it in this section.

First, here are the Korean versions of those actions mentioned earlier.

일어나다, 샤워하다, 먹다, 가다, 공부하다, 일하다, 자다, 쓰다

To use these Korean verbs in conversation, we need to slightly change the forms of the verbs as shown next.

Basic form	Meaning	As used in conversation
일어나다	To wake up	일어나요
샤워하다	To take a shower	샤워해요
먹다	To eat	먹어요
가다	To go	가요
공부하다	To study	공부해요
일하다	To work	일해요
자다	To sleep	자요
쓰다	To write	써요

Tips for changing to conversational form

● If the stem ends with the vowel 아 or 오, add the ending ~아요:
  일어나 + 아요 → 일어**나아** 요 (vowel contraction) → **일어나요**
● If the stem ends with the vowel other than (아 or 오), add the ending ~어요:
  먹 + 어요 → **먹어요**
● If the stem ends with ~하, add the ending ~여요, and then further contract it into 해요:
  공부하 + → 공부하 + 여요 → 공부 (하 + 여 요→ 해요) → **공부해요**
● If the stem ends with a vowel ~ 으, delete the vowel '—' and add ~어요:
  쓰~ + → ㅆ + 어요 → **써요**

[Practice]

Let's practice changing the basic verb forms into the forms used in conversation.

1 맛있다 →
2 맛없다 →
3 좋아하다 →
4 배고프다 →

Make sure that we are all comfortable with changing the forms of verbs/adjectives such that we can use them in conversation. Here, for the sake of convenience we will repeat the verbs/adjectives used in the dialogues of the current lesson:

How do we change the forms such that we can use them in conversation?

1 배고프다 hungry → 배고프 → 배고ㅍ (— deletion) → 배고ㅍ + 아요 → 배고파요
2 먹다 eat → 먹 → 먹 + 어요→ 먹어요
3 좋아하다 like → 좋아하 → 좋아하 + 여요 → 좋아해요
4 맛있다 delicious → 맛있 → 맛있 + 어요 → 맛있어요
5 맛없다 not delicious → 맛없 → 맛없 + 어요 → 맛없어요

Part 2

6 가다 go → 가 → 가 + 아요 → 가아요 (ㅏ deletion) → 가요
7 마시다 drink → 마시 → 마시 + 어요→ 마셔요
8 주문하다 order (something) → 주문하 → 주문하 + 여요 → 주문해요
9 좋다 to be good → 좋 → 좋 + 아요 → 좋아요

Korean verbal conjugation rules:

If the stem vowel is either ㅏ or ㅗ	Add '~아요' to the stem
If the stem vowel is other than ㅏ or ㅗ	Add '~어요' to the stem
If the stem has '하'	Add '~여요' to the stem, then contract (하 + 여요) into 해요

2 ~ 좋아해요? Do you like ~?

Do you like Korean food? Do you like Italian food? How about Chinese food? Here are these expressions in Korean:

한국 음식 좋아해요? Do you like Korean food? (한국 Korean; 음식 food)
이태리 음식 <u>좋아해요</u>? Do you like Italian food? (이태리 Italian)
중국 음식 <u>좋아해요</u>? Do you like Chinese food? (중국 Chinese)
뭐 <u>좋아해요</u>? What do you like? (뭐/무엇 what)
(The wh-question words will be explained in detail in Lesson 4.)

[Practice]

Ask the following questions of your classmates.

1 바나나 좋아해요? (바나나 banana)
2 레몬차 좋아해요? (레몬차 lemon tea)
3 인삼차 좋아해요? (인삼차 ginseng tea)
4 커피 좋아해요? (커피 coffee)
5 불고기 좋아해요? (불고기 Korean-style barbecue)
6 김치 좋아해요? (김치 kimchee)
7 아이스크림 좋아해요? (아이스크림 ice cream)

3 이게/저게 뭐예요? What is this? What is that?

When you are curious about something, you start asking questions: "What is this? What is that?" Ask the same questions, now, in Korean as follows:

<u>이게</u> 뭐예요? What is <u>this</u>?
<u>저게</u> 뭐예요? What is <u>that</u>?

Demonstratives (이게, 저게, 그게) will be further explained in the later chapters. In this chapter, we will begin by practicing 이게 and 저게, as shown next.

이게 (this)	이게 indicates something that is **closer** to the **speaker**.
저게 (that)	저게 indicates something that is **away** from both **speaker** and **listener**.

52

Lesson 2: Meals and foods 식사와 음식

Video clip

Here is a sample dialogue.

레이첼: 이게 뭐예요? What is this?
윤호: 커피예요. (커피 coffee)
레이첼: 저게 뭐예요? What is that?
윤호: 레몬차예요. (레몬차 lemon tea)
레이첼: 그럼, 저게 뭐예요? What is that?
윤호: 녹차예요. (녹차 green tea)

[Practice]

Using the clues provided, answer the following questions as shown in the example.

[Example]

    이게 뭐예요? → (공책 notebook): 공책이에요.
1 이게 뭐예요? → (컴퓨터 computer): _____.
2 저게 뭐예요? → (의자 chair): _____.
3 저게 뭐예요? → (시계 clock): _____.

4 햄버거가 맛있어요. Subject particle

In Lesson 1, we talked about the particle (or marker) '~는' (as in 저는 탐이에요 I am Tom), and we will now discuss another particle '~가' (as in 햄버거가 맛있어요 Hamburgers are delicious). The particle '~가' is called the subject particle because the particle '~가' indicates its preceding noun is the subject (i.e. the doer of the action) in a sentence. Depending on the noun-ending form, it has a variant '~이' as shown below.

1 햄버거가 맛있어요. Hamburgers are delicious.
2 김치가 맛있어요. Kimchi is delicious.

53

Part 2

3 불고기가 맛있어요. Bulgogi is delicious.
4 비빔밥이 맛있어요. Bibimbap is delicious.
5 아이스크림이 맛있어요. Ice cream is delicious.
6 삼계탕이 맛있어요. Chicken-ginseng soup is delicious.

The nouns in (1) through (3) end with a vowel in Korean; the particle ~가 is added while the nouns in (4) through (6) all end with a consonant, which is followed by ~이. The function of the two variants ('~가/이') is the same, and the selection of each form depends on the preceding noun forms (either vowel-ending or consonant-ending). This variation of the form is for the ease of pronunciation.

Here is the summary of this variation of the subject particle ~가/이:

If the subject noun ends with a vowel:	Then, add the subject particle ~가 (햄버거가 맛있어요)
If the subject noun ends with a consonant:	Then, add the subject particle ~이 (비빔밥이 맛있어요)

[Practice]

Fill in blanks with the correct subject particle variant form (~가 or ~이).

1 샌드위치 _____ 맛있어요. Sandwiches are delicious.
2 파인애플 _____ 맛있어요. Pineapples are delicious.
3 커피 _____ 맛있어요. Coffee is delicious.
4 레몬차 _____ 맛있어요. Lemon tea is delicious.

5 음식도 also/too

Linda likes apples, and she also likes bananas. She is crazy about oranges, as well. How do you express these ideas in Korean? That is easy:

린다는 사과 좋아해요. Linda likes apples.
린다는 바나나도 좋아해요. Linda likes bananas, <u>too</u>.
린다는 오렌지도 좋아해요. Linda likes oranges, <u>too</u>.

Here we will introduce another particle '~도' which can be translated as "also, too, or as well" in English. As shown above, by adding this particle '~도' to the preceding nouns (here, 바나나도 banana, 오렌지도 orange), we express that the subject, *Linda*, likes apples, and she likes bananas, too (= 바나나도 좋아해요). She also likes oranges (= 오렌지도 좋아해요).

[Practice]

Say what you like using the particle ~도 in response to the question "뭐 좋아해요?"

Question: 뭐 좋아해요? (뭐 = 무엇 what)
Answer: 저는 커피 좋아해요.

1 저는 _____ 좋아해요.
2 저는 _____ 좋아해요.
3 저는 _____ 좋아해요.
4 저는 _____ 좋아해요.

54

Lesson 2: Meals and foods 식사와 음식

6 카페테리아에 가요. Destination particle

In this chapter, you saw that Rachel and Yoon-ho were hungry after the new student orientation. They wanted to grab something to eat, so they went to the school cafeteria. At this moment, you too get hungry and you want to go to the cafeteria for a sandwich or something, right? Before you go, we want to focus on the structure *you* or (someone) go to [some place] and, for that, we add another particle, '~에', which is called the "destination" particle because it indicates the place you are going when using the verb '가다' (to go). Following are some sample sentences.

1 저는 학교에 가요. (학교 school)
2 저는 학교 카페테리아에 가요. (카페테리아 cafeteria)
3 저는 학교 도서관에 가요. (도서관 library)
4 저는 학교 체육관에 가요. (체육관 gym)
  → 저는 [place] + 에 (to "destination") 가요 (가다 to go).

The "destination particle" is not new to us. For example, we use "to" which indicates where we are going as in "I go <u>to</u> the library." Unlike English, however, the destination particle is situated *after* the noun for destination (not before the noun) in Korean as shown:

I go <u>to</u> the library.
저는 도서관<u>에</u> 가요.

With the question word 어디 ("where") you can ask where someone is headed to. Here is a conversation between Michael and Damee.

Dami: 마이클 씨, 어디에 가요? Michael, where are you going?
Michael: 도서관에 가요. 다미 씨는 어디에 가요? I am going to the library. And you?
Dami: 저도 도서관에 가요. I am also going to the library.

[Practice]

Ask the question "어디에 가요?" of your classmates. They will answer the question using the following clues:

  You ask 어디에 가요?
1 Classmate 1: 학교 → _____
2 Classmate 2: 식당 → _____
3 Classmate 3: 교실 → _____
4 Classmate 4: 기숙사 → _____
5 Classmate 5: 커피숍→ _____
  (학교 school; 식당 restaurant; 교실 classroom; 기숙사 dormitory; 커피숍 coffee shop)

7 그리고 and/그럼 then

In this chapter, we will learn how to connect the ideas in two sentences using the sentence connectives 그리고 (and) or 그럼 (then).

  Sentence 1 **그리고** Sentence 2
  Sentence 1 **그럼** Sentence 2

55

Part 2

1 그리고 – This sentence connective is used to link two or more related sentences as shown:

린다는 커피 좋아해요. **그리고** (린다는) 레몬차도 좋아해요. **그리고** 녹차도 좋아해요.
Linda likes coffee. AND she also likes lemon tea. AND she likes green tea, too.

2 그럼 – The sentence connective 그럼 is translated as "then":

소라: 이게 뭐예요? What is this?
제니퍼: 커피예요. It is coffee.
소라: 그럼 , 저게 뭐예요? THEN, what is that?

8 하나, 둘, 셋, 넷, 다섯 Counting numbers in Korean: Native-Korean numbers

One of the challenges in learning Korean is to learn how to count because Korean has two different number systems (i.e., Native-Korean numbers and Sino-Korean or Chinese-originated numbers) depending on what you count. In this chapter, we will introduce the Native-Korean numbers and then count one to five using the native number system. The following table shows how to count to 5 using Native-Korean numbers.

1	2	3	4	5
하나	둘	셋	넷	다섯

Repeat these native numbers one more time: 하나 – 둘 – 셋 – 넷 – 다섯. The following illustration shows how to count cups of coffee using the native numbers.

One to five cups of hot drink
Image created by authors with pixabay image

'잔' is the counter word for "cup," and 한 잔 means "a cup of coffee," which indicates a combination of 1 (using the Native-Korean number) plus '잔,' which is the counter for cup in Korean. Let's count up to five cups of coffee as shown in the pictures. Here you notice that the forms of the numbers look a little different with the counter '잔'.

Lesson 2: Meals and foods 식사와 음식

Number	Number + Counter '잔'
하나 (1)	한 잔 One cup of a hot beverage
둘 (2)	두 잔 Two cups of a hot beverage
셋 (3)	세 잔 Three cups a hot beverage
넷 (4)	네 잔 Four cups a hot beverage
다섯 (5)	다섯 잔 Five cups of a hot beverage

Given this, let's practice more by counting (1) persons, (2) animals, (3) books, and (4) items/things. First, we need to know more counters for person, animal, book, and item/thing as shown.

Table 2.1 More counters for person, animal, book, and item

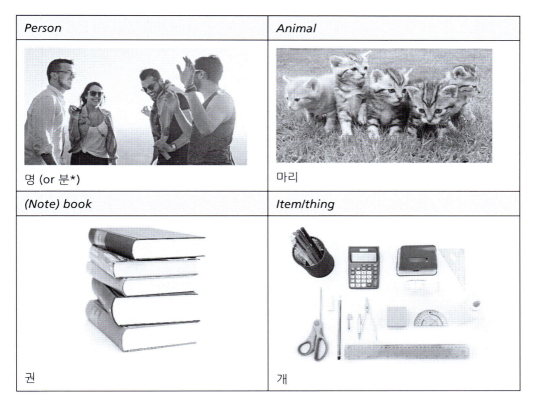

Person	Animal
명 (or 분*)	마리
(Note) book	Item/thing
권	개

Pixabay.com

The counter '분' is used over '명' when you want to sound polite when counting persons. Politeness in language use is important in Korean, and we will talk more about ways in which the Korean language is used later in this textbook series.

57

Part 2

Now let's count up to five persons, animals or things with the specific counters.

Person	Animal
한 명 (한 분)	한 마리
두 명 (두 분)	두 마리
세 명 (세 분)	세 마리
네 명 (네 분)	네 마리
다섯 명 (다섯 분)	다섯 마리
Book	Item (e.g., school supplies)
한 권	한 개
두 권	두 개
세 권	세 개
네 권	네 개
다섯 권	다섯 개

We will learn more numbers in Lesson 4.

Lesson 2: Meals and foods 식사와 음식

Activity 1

Introducing favorite foods

Introduce your favorite food to your friends!

여러분은 어떤 종류의 음식을 좋아해요? What kind of food do you like?
그 음식을 반 친구들에게 소개해 봅시다. Let's introduce the food to our classmates!
다음의 음식 사진을 보고 이름을 이야기해 보세요. Talk about the food of following pictures.

Mandu (만두, Korean dumpling)
Pixabay.com

Pizza (피자)
Pixabay.com

Rice noodle (쌀국수)
Pixabay.com

Part 2

Activity 2

Inquiring about the food

1 여러분이 준비한 메뉴판을 교실의 벽에 붙이세요. Put your menu on the walls of classroom.

2 친구들의 메뉴판을 보면서 물어보세요. Look at your friend's menu, and ask questions.

- 이 음식에 _____ (e.g., 치즈) 있어요? Does this food contain _____ (e.g., cheese)?
- 이 음식에 _____ (e.g., 토마토) 없어요? This food doesn't contain t _____, does it (e.g., tomato)?
- 맛있어요? 맛없어요? Is it delicious? not-delicious?

3 가장 맛있게 보이는 메뉴판에 투표하세요. Vote on your favorite menu.

Lesson 2: Meals and foods 식사와 음식

Cultural notes

Ordering food in Korean

Do you want to try delicious food in a Korean restaurant? Or do you want to call up a delivery service to order food? Once you've figured out where you want to eat out, walk right in and sit down where you'd like. Most casual dining places in Korea are first-come, first-serve, so you just walk in and sit where you want. In a family restaurant or fancy restaurant, however, you might want to wait for a server to offer you a seat. What is the appropriate way to order food in Korea? When you are ready to order or want to get a server's attention, call for the waiter or waitress by saying "여기요". The server will then come over to take your order. To order the food you've chosen, say the name of food plus the number of orders plus 주세요 (주세요 means "give something"). For example, if you want a couple of rolls of kimbap, you can say, 김밥 두 개 (two) 주세요, which means "Please give me two rolls of kimbap." To change the number of servings, pair a Sino-Korean number with 인분 (~인분 roughly means "servings"). For example, one serving 일 인분, two servings 이 인분, three servings 삼 인분, four servings 사 인분, five servings 오 인분, six servings 육 인분, and so on. Shortly after you have ordered, you will be served an assortment of small side dishes called 반찬, which may include kimchi (김치 traditional fermented cabbage) or kkakdugi (깍두기|fermented radish). Typically, 김치 is made from napa cabbage and fermented with seasonings like Korean chili powder, salt, green onion, and garlic. When you are done eating and want to pay, walk toward the cash register, or wait for the server to give you the bill. Say 계산할게요, "I'd like to pay my bill." Traditionally, Korean people tend to treat their companions, often fighting over the bill. If one person insists on paying for everyone, you can pay next time.

Hot and spicy rice cake

Do you like Korean food? Do you want to learn to make Korean food at home? If you are new to Korean cooking, you can start with asnack food made from soft rice cakes (떡) and red pepper paste (고추장). You can find most of these ingredients at an Asian market or Korean market.

Recipe

Ingredients

One pound of rice cakes
Four cups of water
Seven large dried anchovies
One-third cup hot pepper paste
One tablespoon sugar
One tablespoon hot pepper flakes
Three green onions, cut into three-inch-long pieces
Two hard-boiled eggs
One-half pound fish cakes (optional)

Directions

1 Add the water and dried anchovies to a shallow pot or pan.
2 Boil for 15 minutes over medium high heat without the lid.

Part 2

3 Combine the hot pepper paste, flakes, and sugar in a small bowl.
4 Remove the anchovies from the pot and add the rice cakes, green onion, eggs, and optional fish cakes.
5 When the mixture starts to boil, stir gently until the rice cakes become soft and the sauce thickens and looks shiny (about 10–15 minutes).
6 Remove from the heat and serve hot.

Recipe from **www.maangchi.com**

떡볶이, Hot and spicy rice cake
https://pixabay.com/en/toppokki-food-korean-food-1607479/

Vocabulary expansion

밑줄 친 단어를 보세요. 상자 안에 있는 단어를 사용해서 다음의 대화를 연습하세요. Please look at the underlined words. Use the words in the box to practice the following conversations.

Ordering food

윤호:　레이첼 씨, 같이 **아침** 먹어요.
레이첼:　좋아요. 뭐 먹어요?
윤호:　시리얼 먹어요.
레이첼:　저는 **토스트** 먹어요.
윤호:　그래요? 그럼 저는 **오믈렛** 도 먹어요.

62

Lesson 2: Meals and foods 식사와 음식

Vocabulary

아침 breakfast
시리얼 cereal
토스트 toast
오믈렛 omelet

아침 메뉴 breakfast menu

점심 lunch
중국 음식 Chinese food
볶음밥 fried rice
짜장면 black-bean noodles
탕수육 sweet and sour pork

중국 음식 메뉴 Chinese food menu

저녁 dinner
멕시코 음식 Mexican food
타코 taco
부리또 burrito

멕시코 음식 메뉴 Mexican food menu

Lesson 3

School life 학교 생활

Learning goals

- Talk about courses you are currently taking.
- Ask about the location of your classes.

Grammar and expressions

- 알아요/몰라요. I know/I don't know.
- 빅뱅이요. Noun + (이)요: Respond with a short answer forms.
- 한국어를 잘 하고 싶어요. I want to . . .
- 한국어 수업을 들어 보세요. Suggestions "Why don't you . . .?"
- 듣다/들어요. Irregular verbs in Korean
- 그런데. By the way, however/그래서 Therefore, thus
- 수학 수업은 어디에서 해요? Where is the Math class?
- 어때요?, 괜찮아요, 그래요? Very useful expressions

Activities

- Poster fair
- Weekly class schedules

Part 2

Cultural notes
- Universities in Korea
- K-pop

Vocabulary expansion
- Words for majors at college

DIALOGUE 1

Do you know? 알아요?

Yoon-ho recommends that Rachel take a Korean language class.

레이첼: 윤호 씨, 혹시 빅뱅 알아요?
윤호: 빅뱅이요? 알아요. 왜요?
레이첼: 제가 케이-팝을 정말 좋아해요.
윤호: 아, 그래요?
레이첼: 네. 그래서 한국어를 잘하고 싶어요.
윤호: 그럼, 한국어 수업을 들어 보세요.
레이첼: 한국어 수업이요?
윤호: 네, 이번 학기에 한국어 일 학년 수업이 있어요. 한번 들어 보세요.

Video clip

Lesson 3: School life 학교 생활

Word check-up

혹시 或是	(adv.)	by any chance
알아요 (알다)	(v.)	to know
왜요?		Why?
제가ㅣ		(honorific/first person)
케이-팝		K-pop, Korean pop culture
정말	(adv.)	really
좋아해요 (좋아하다)	(v.)	to like
그래서		thus, therefore
한국어	(n.)	Korean language
잘하다		do something well
~고 싶어요		want (like) to (do something)
그럼	(conn.)	then
수업 授業	(n.)	class
일 一	(n.)	one (number)
학년 學年	(n.)	year/grade
이번		this time
학기 學期	(n.)	semester
있어요		informal/present form of 있다
있다		to be, there is, to have
한번 -番	(adv.)	once
듣다 (들어요)	(v.)	to listen, to hear
~아/어 보세요		try out to

Rachel: Yoon-ho, do you know BIGBANG by any chance?
Yoon-ho: BIGBANG? I know them. Why?
Rachel: I really like K-pop.
Yoon-ho: Ah, is that so?
Rachel: Yes. So I want to speak Korean very well.
Yoon-ho: Then, think about taking a Korean class.
Rachel: Korean class?
Yoon-ho: Yes, there is a first-year Korean class offered this semester. You should try to take it.

Part 2

DIALOGUE 2

How about? 어때요?

Yoon-ho and Rachel discuss classes they are taking this semester.

레이첼: 윤호 씨, 이번 학기에 뭐 공부해요?
윤호: 저는 수학, 심리학, 사회학, 그리고 경제학 수업을 들어요.
레이첼: 아, 그래요? 수학 수업은 어때요?
윤호: 괜찮아요. 그런데, 숙제가 많아요.
레이첼: 수학 수업은 어디에서 해요?
윤호: 밴 하이즈에서 해요. 레이첼 씨, 한국어 수업은 어디에서 해요?
레이첼: 한국어 수업도 밴 하이즈에서 해요.
윤호: 한국어 수업은 어때요?
레이첼: 아주 재미있어요. 그리고 선생님도 친절해요. 그런데 한국어 발음이 조금 어려워요.

Lesson 3: School life 학교 생활

Word check-up

무엇 (뭐)		what
공부 工夫	(n.)	study
수학 數學	(n.)	Mathematics
심리학 心理學	(n.)	Psychology
사회학 社會學	(n.)	Sociology
경제학 經濟學	(n.)	Economics
들어요		informal/present form of 듣다
어때요?		How is it?
괜찮아요		It is okay.
숙제 宿題	(n.)	homework/assignments
많아요 (많다)		many/much
어디	(adv.)	where
~에서	(part.)	from ~/at (a place)
그런데	(conn.)	but/however/by the way
아주	(adv.)	very
재미있어요 (재미있다)	(adj.)	to be interesting/fun
그리고		and
선생님 先生-	(n.)	teacher
친절해요 (친절하다) 親切-	(adj.)	to be kind
발음 發音	(n.)	pronunciation
조금	(adv.)	little/few
어려워요 (어렵다)	(adj.)	to be difficult
밴 하이즈		name of a campus building

Rachel: What are you studying this semester, Yoon-ho?
Yoon-ho: I am taking Mathematics, Psychology, Sociology, and Economics.
Rachel: Ah, really? How is the Mathematics class?
Yoon-ho: It's okay, but it has a lot of assignments.
Rachel: Where is your Math class?
Yoon-ho: It's in Van Hise. Rachel, where do you have Korean class?
Rachel: My Korean class is in Van Hise as well.
Yoon-ho: How is the Korean class?
Rachel: It's very interesting and the teacher is very kind, but Korean pro-
          nunciation is a little difficult.

Part 2

Grammar and expressions

1 알아요/몰라요. I know/I don't know

The expression "알아요" is used when the speaker confirms that he/she is aware of the fact being presented. As a question, this expression asks whether or not the listener is aware or informed of the situation as shown in the following example:

레이첼: 빅뱅 알아요? Do you know the K-Pop group, BIGBANG?
윤호: 네, 알아요. Yes, I do.

If you are not aware nor informed, then, you can answer by saying "몰라요," which is the opposite of "알아요". It essentially means, "No, I don't know."

민지: 마이클 씨 알아요? Do you know Michael? (= Have you met Michael?)
탐: 아니요, 몰라요. No, I don't. (= No, I haven't met him.)

Quick check-up of verbal conjugation

Let's quickly check the conjugations of "알아요/몰라요" from the basic forms, 알다/모르다, respectively.

- 알다 to know → The stem (or root) is 알 and its stem vowel is ㅏ. Following the conjugation rule, if the stem vowel is either ㅏ or ㅗ, then, the ending '~아요' is added to the stem. If you are sure about this, go check Lesson 2, the stem 알~ is followed by the ending 아요.

  알~ (step 1: check out the stem vowel) → + 아요 (step 2: since the stem vowel is ㅏ, the ending '아요' is attached) → 알아요 (the final conjugation form, which is the form used in conversation)

- 모르다 not know → The stem ends with ~르. This is one of irregular verbs so called '르' – irregular because the stem final 르 goes through a transformation during conjugation. Let's find out, step-by-step.

  모르~ (Step 1: Check out the stem which ends with ~ 르) → 모ㄹ (Step 2: the stem vowel ㅡ is deleted) → 몰ㄹ (Step 3: add another ㄹ ending up with the double 'ㄹㄹ' → 몰ㄹ + 아요 (Step 4: Due to the vowel deletion, the stem vowel is now 'ㅗ' as in '모'. Thus, the ending ~아요 is attached) → 몰라요 (the final conversational form).

- 모르다 is one of the '르-irregular verbs'. Here are more examples of the '르-irregular verbs'.

Step 1	Step 2	Step 3	Step 4	Step 5
부르 – 다 to call	부 ㄹ	불 ㄹ	불ㄹ + 어요	불러요
기르 – 다 to raise (animals)	기 ㄹ	길 ㄹ	길ㄹ + 어요	길러요
다르 – 다 to be different	다 ㄹ	달 ㄹ	달ㄹ + 아요	달라요

2 빅뱅이요. Noun + (이)요: Respond with a short answer form.

When you are asked, you can simply answer with a short answer as shown here.

Michael: What is your name?
Tom: Tom. (Or, you can say "I am Tom," or "My name is Tom.")

70

Lesson 3: School life 학교 생활

In the same way, you can answer the question with a short answer in Korean.

마이클: 이름이 뭐예요?
탐: 탐이요.
마이클: 이름이 뭐예요?
안나: 안나요.

탐 + 이요	← When the name ends with a consonant
안나 + 요	← When the name ends with a vowel

As shown, the short answer is the combination of [noun] + (이)요; there is a slight variation depending on the noun ending. If the noun ends with a consonant (e.g., Tom 탐), then [noun]+이요; if the noun ends with a vowel (e.g., Anna 안나), then, [noun] + 요. This variation of the short answer form is mainly for ease of pronunciation in Korean.

[Practice 1]

Fill in the blanks with either ~이요 or ~요 for short answers.

Question: 이름이 뭐예요?

1 사라 → 사라 _____.
2 민영 → 민영 _____.
3 레이첼 → 레이첼 _____.

[Practice 2]

Answer the following questions with the short answer forms.

1 전화번호 (telephone number) 뭐예요?
2 이-메일 (email) 뭐예요?

3   한국어를 잘 하고 싶어요. I want to . . .

You often find yourself in the situation where you want to express "I want to do (something) or I want to go (somewhere)." The linguistic structure consists of your desire "I want to . . ." plus certain actions expressed by certain verbs (e.g., I want to study; I want to eat; I want to go). In a similar way, you can say "I want to do something" in Korean by using the combination of expressions '~고 싶다' as shown.

I want to	Study	I want to study
~고 싶다	공부하다	공부하고 싶어요
I want to	eat	I want to eat
~고 싶다	먹다	먹고 싶어요
I want to	go	I want to go
~고 싶다	가다	가고 싶어요

71

Part 2

You can now say specifically that you want to (1) study, (2) eat, and (3) go, as shown here.

1 한국어를 <u>공부하고 싶어요</u>. I want to study the Korean language.
2 불고기를 <u>먹고 싶어요</u>. I want to eat bulgogi (Korean-style barbecue).
3 서울에 <u>가고 싶어요</u>. I want to go to Seoul (the capital of South Korea).

Here is a sample conversation between Michael and Dami using the structure ~고 싶어요.

마이클: 안녕하세요, 다미 씨?
다미: 안녕하세요, 마이클 씨?
마이클: 아, 배고파요 (I am hungry). 햄버거 먹고 싶어요.
다미: 저도 햄버거 먹고 싶어요.
마이클: 그럼, 같이 학교 카페테리아에 가요.
다미: 좋아요.

[Practice]

Answer the following question using ~고 싶어요.

1 뭐 먹고 싶어요?
2 뭐 공부하고 싶어요?
3 어디에 가고 싶어요?

Question words in Korean: 뭐 (= 무엇) what, 어디 where.

4 한국어 수업을 들어 보세요. Suggestions: "Why don't you take a Korean class?"

You want to suggest something new for your classmates to try out, but you don't want to sound "pushy." Here is a perfect way of doing that in Korean using the structure ~어 보세요. In Lesson 2, we learned how to conjugate some verbs, and we repeat the same verbs here (먹다, 공부하다, 가다, 쓰다) along with a new verb '듣다' for this structure.

Basic form	Conjugation	With ~어 보세요
먹다 to eat	먹어요	먹어 보세요 (먹어요 + 보세요)
공부하다 to study	공부해요	공부해 보세요 (공부해요 + 보세요)
가다 to go	가요	가 보세요 (가요 + 보세요)
쓰다 to write	써요	써 보세요 (써요 + 보세요)
듣다 to take a course; to listen to	들어요	들어 보세요 (들어요 + 보세요)

[Practice]

With ~어 보세요, you politely suggest or propose something new to your classmates:

1 불고기를 <u>먹어 보세요</u>. Why don't you try Bulgogi?
2 한국어를 <u>공부해 보세요</u>. Why don't you study Korean?
3 서울에 <u>가 보세요</u>. Why don't you go to Seoul?
4 한국어를 <u>들어 보세요</u>. Why don't you take a Korean class?

72

Lesson 3: School life 학교 생활

5 듣다/들어요. Irregular verbs in Korean

'듣다' needs special attention because the stem-final consonant changes in conjugation (i.e., ㄷ → ㄹ). We call this an ㄷ – irregular form.

● 듣 – 다 → Step 1 (듣 + 어요) → Step 2 (듣 becomes 들 (ㄷ → ㄹ) before the ending ~어요) → 들어요

There are additional verbs that go through similar steps:

● 걷 – 다 to walk → 걷 + 어요 → 걸 + 어요→ 걸어요 I walk
● 묻 – 다 to ask → 묻 + 어요 → 물 + 어요→ 물어요 I ask (something)

Thus far we have seen some irregular verbs in Korean. By "irregular verbs," we mean that the stem (or root) is changed for conjugation (e.g., 듣다 → 들어요 (ㄷ → ㄹ: ㄷ – irregular); 모르다 → 몰라요 (르 → ㄹㄹ: 르 – irregular). Now we'll introduce another kind of irregular verbs called ㅂ-irregular.

ㅂ-irregular conjugation

● Step 1: 어렵다 (to be difficult, hard)
● Step 2: 어렵 + 어요: add ~어요 to the stem (or root) '어렵 –'
● Step 3: 어려 + (ㅂ → ㅜ) + 어요: the stem-final 'ㅂ' turns to ㅜ before ~어요
● Step 4: 어려워요: the conjugated form

Here are more examples of ㅂ-irregular forms:

● 춥다 (to be cold) → 춥 + 어요 → 추 + (ㅂ → ㅜ) + 어요→ 추워요
● 덥다 (to be warm) → 덥 + 어요 → 더 + (ㅂ → ㅜ) + 어요→ 더워요
● 쉽다 (to be easy) → 쉽 + 어요 → 쉬 + (ㅂ → ㅜ) + 어요→ 쉬워요
● 돕다 (to help) → 돕 + 아요 → 도 + (ㅂ → ㅗ) + 아요→ 도와요

By now, you may have started to think that there are quite a few irregular forms to remember in Korean. Actually, *how many more are there?* Well, you will probably think differently when you recall that English also has quite a few irregular or exceptional forms for past-tense verbs. For example, I usually take a bus to school. However, yesterday I was late for school, so I took a taxi. I should have taken the subway instead, because the traffic was horrible.

Here is the summary table of the irregular forms we've talked about.

으 – irregular: 쓰다 write (a letter)	쓰 +어요 → ㅆ + 어요→ 써요
르 – irregular: 모르다 do not know	모르 + 아요 → 몰ㄹ + 아요→ 몰라요
ㄷ – irregular: 듣다 listen (to music)	듣 + 어요→ 듣→들 +어요→ 들어요
ㅂ – irregular: 춥다 cold	춥 + 어요→ 추 + ㅜ + 어요→ 추워요

6 그런데 by the way, however ; 그래서 therefore, thus

If you recall, we studied the two sentence connectives, 그리고 and 그럼 in Lesson 2:

린다는 커피 좋아해요. Linda likes coffee.
그리고 레몬차도 좋아해요. <u>AND</u> she likes lemon tea.

73

Part 2

마이클: 이게 뭐예요? What is this?
사라: 커피예요. It is coffee.
마이클: <u>그럼</u>, 저게 뭐예요? <u>THEN</u>, what is that?

In this chapter, we will introduce additional sentence connectives, 그런데 and 그래서.

1 **그런데**: This connective is translated as "in contrast, however, but" or "by the way," depending on the context as shown in the following list.

윤호: 한국어 수업은 어때요? How's your Korean class?
사라: 재미있어요. <u>그런데</u>, 숙제가 많아요. It is fun. However, there are a lot of homework assignments.
마이클: 아, 피곤해요. <u>그런데</u> 지금 뭐 해요? I am tired. By the way, what are you doing now?
탐: 지금 한국어 숙제해요. I am doing my Korean homework.

2 **그래서**: This connective is used to connect two sentences and is translated as "therefore," "so," "thus," or "as a result."

오늘은 아주 피곤해요. **그래서** 집에 가고 싶어요. I am very tired today. Thus, I want to go home.

Summary of sentence connectives:

- 그리고 And,
- 그럼 Then,
- 그런데 However, by the way
- 그래서 Therefore, thus, so

6 수학 수업은 어디에서 해요? Where is the Math class?

윤호: 한국어 수업은 어디에서 해요. Where is the Korean class?
레이첼: 밴 하이즈요. In Van Hise.
윤호: 그럼, 수학 수업은 어디에서 해요? Then, where is your Math class?
레이첼: 수학 수업도 밴 하이즈에서 해요. It is also in Van Hise.

In Lesson 2 you were introduced to a destination particle ~에, which usually goes with the verb 가다 (to go), indicating you are going to a certain place as shown here.

마이클: 어디에 가요?
탐: 저는 도서관에 가요. (도서관 library)
제인: 저는 교실에 가요. (교실 classroom)
다미: 저는 체육관에 가요. (체육관 gym)

In this section, we will introduce another location or place particle: '~에서': The location particle ~에서 is needed to express the location/place where a certain action takes place. The motion verbs such as 가다 (to go) and 오다 (to come) involve movement toward the certain place or destination whereas some action verbs (such as study, eat, drink, etc.) denote active actions that are taking place in a certain place. Here are some examples:

1 마이클 씨는 도서관에서 공부해요.
2 마이클 씨는 식당에서 먹어요.
3 마이클 씨는 커피숍에서 커피 마셔요.

Lesson 3: School life 학교 생활

4 마이클 씨는 실험실에서 연습해요 (실험실 laboratory; 연습하다 practice).

→ 마이클 씨는 [place] + 에서 (= in the place) does something.

[Practice]

Ask your classmates about the location of their favorite class using "어디에서 해요?" Then your partner will answer the question with [place] + '에서 해요'.

[Example]

한국어 수업은 어디에서 해요?
→ 한국어 수업은 밴 하이즈에서 해요.

1 수학 수업은 어디에서 해요? (수학 수업 Math class) →
2 과학 수업은 어디에서 해요? (과학 수업 Science class) →
3 영어 수업은 어디에서 해요? (영어 수업 English class) →
4 컴퓨터 수업은 어디에서 해요? (컴퓨터 수업 computer class) →

7 어때요?, 괜찮아요, 그래요? Very useful expressions

In Lesson 3, here are some very useful expressions that Koreans often use in conversation:

1 *어때요?*: In a question, the expression "어때요?" asks about the listener's opinion or thoughts on the situation or topic being talked about. It can be translated as "How do you like . . .?"
2 *괜찮아요*: The expression "괜찮아요" can be translated "It is fine/okay" or "It is not bad." Koreans use this expression quite often instead of saying "좋아요," especially when they express their opinions or thoughts on things, situations. or people indirectly. In that sense, depending on the situation, the expression "괜찮아요" can work quite well.
3 *그래요?*: During a conversation, the listener may respond to the speaker by saying "그래요?" as a way of showing that he/she is paying attention to the speaker while not interrupting the flow of the conversation. Or, if you want to ascertain if what you are told is true, you may also use this expression as a question.

윤호: 레이첼 씨, 안녕하세요? 수학 수업은 **어때요**? Hi, Rachel. How do you like your Math class?
레이첼: **괜찮아요**. It is fine.
윤호: **그래요**? 한국어 수업은 **어때요**? Is that so? How about your Korean class?
레이첼: 아주 재미있어요. It is quite fun.
윤호: 아, **그래요**? Ah, is that right?

75

Part 2

Activity 1

Poster fair

Do you have a favorite festival? Does your hometown have a popular festival? You will present your favorite festivals to your classmates. Bring posters of the festivals. During the poster fair session, you will talk about your favorite festivals with your classmates.

Sample questions

1 재즈 축제 (Jazz Festival) 알아요? 한번 가 보세요.
2 밀워키 여름 축제 (Milwaukee Summer Festival) 알아요? 한번 가 보세요.
3 르네상스 축제 (Renaissance Festival) 알아요? 한번 가 보세요.

Activity 2

Weekly class schedules

Which courses are you taking this semester? Make a weekly schedule along with times and locations. In a group, take turns asking and answering questions about your weekly schedules.

Ask your partner questions!

Q: 이번 학기에 뭐 공부해요?
A: 한국어 수업 들어요.
Q: 한국어 수업은 어디에서 해요?
A: 밴 하이즈에 548교실에서 해요.
Q: 한국어 수업은 어때요?
A: 아주 재미있어요. 그리고 선생님도 친절해요. 그런데 한국어 발음이 조금 어려워요.

Video clip

Part 2

Cultural notes

Universities in Korea

After taking the Korean college entrance exam, Korean high school students enter universities. Currently, there are more than 370 official higher education providers, including 179 private universities and 43 national universities. The highest ranked university in South Korea, Seoul National University, is placed 36th in the World University Rankings and tenth in the University Rankings in Asia (from topuniversities.com). Seoul National University is one of the three prestigious so-called *SKY* universities, which also include Korea University and Yonsei University in Seoul. Located in Daejeon, KAIST (Korea Advanced Institute of Science and Technology) is the second-highest ranked Korean institution. KAIST was established as the nation's first research-led science and engineering institution. POSTECH (Pohang University of Science and Technology) also offers a science and technology-focused curriculum. POSTECH is the first South Korean university to be officially labeled a bilingual campus in both Korean and English.

The school year is divided into two terms, the first academic term and the second academic term. The first term usually runs from the first Monday of February to mid June, upon which the summer recess begins and continues until late August. The second term usually resumes in late August and runs until mid December. The winter break is from late December to late January. There are two exams: the mid-term and the final. In 2004, the South Korean government set a target of attracting more than 100,000 foreign students to its universities by 2012, and by 2011 the country had enrolled over 85,000 international students from 171 different countries.

K-pop

K-pop (abbreviation of "Korean popular music" or "Korean pop") is a musical genre originating in South Korea. K-pop includes dance-pop, pop ballad, electronic, rock, metal, hip-hop music, and R&B. Modern K-pop was ushered in with the 1992 debut of Seo Taiji and Boys (서태지와 아이들). Their song "I Know" (난 알아요) sparked a paradigm shift in the music industry of South Korea. K-pop culture is becoming an increasingly globalized phenomenon called *Hallyu* (Korean Wave, 한류) worldwide.[1]

Vocabulary expansion

밑줄 친 단어를 보세요. 상자 안에 있는 단어를 사용해서 다음의 대화를 연습하세요. Please look at the underlined words. Use the words in the box to practice the following conversations.

What is your major?

윤호: 레이첼 씨, 전공이 뭐예요?
레이첼: **간호학** 이에요.
윤호: 그래요? 그럼 이번 학기에 뭐 공부해요?
레이첼: **노인 환자** 수업을 들어요.
윤호: 정말요? 그 수업은 어때요?

Lesson 3: School life 학교 생활

Students of various majors in the lecture hall
Pixabay.com
University lecture hall

Vocabulary

전공	major(s)
간호학	*Nursing*
노인환자	senior patients
병원	hospital
간호사	nurse
교육학	*Education*
초등학생	elementary school student
초등학교	elementary school
선생님	teacher
식품과학	*Nutritional science*
비타민	vitamin
식품회사	food company
연구원	researcher

Note

1 www.wattpad.com/160840854-k-pop-groups-intro-to-k-pop

Lesson 4

Dating 데이트하기

Learning goals

- Ask for the time of day and for phone numbers.
- Ask about the price of certain items.

Grammar and expressions

- 시간 있어요? Are you available? Do you have free time?
- 몇 시예요? What time is it?
- 게임이 몇 시에 있어요? What time is the game?
- 윤호 씨하고 같이 가고 싶어요. I want to go with Yoon-ho.
- 제 전화번호는 123-4567이에요. My phone number is 123-4567.
- 지금 어디예요? Where are you now?
- 얼마예요? How much is it?
- 여기 있어요. Here it is.

Activities

- My dating plan 1
- My dating plan 2

Part 2

Cultural notes
- Korean currency, "won"
- Korea–Yonsei varsity games

Vocabulary expansion
- Words for sports

DIALOGUE 1

Do you have time? 시간 있어요?

Yoon-ho and Rachel exchange cell phone numbers after deciding to go on a date this weekend.

레이첼: 윤호 씨, 주말에 시간 있어요?

윤호: 네. 시간 있어요.

레이첼: 혹시 미식축구 좋아해요?

윤호: 네. 아주 좋아해요. 미식축구 팬이에요. 왜요?

레이첼: 이번 토요일에 뱃져스 (Badgers) 게임이 있어요. 그래서 윤호 씨 하고 같이 가고 싶어요.

윤호: 좋아요! 게임이 몇 시에 있어요?

레이첼: 토요일 오후 두(2) 시에 있어요.

윤호: 좋아요. 같이 가요. 아, 핸드폰 번호가 뭐예요?

레이첼: 987–6543이에요. 윤호 씨는요?

윤호: 제 전화번호는 123–4567이에요. 그럼 토요일에 만나요.

Lesson 4: Dating 데이트하기

Word check-up

주말 週末	(n.)	weekend
시간 時間	(n.)	time
있어요? (있다)	(v.)	have (do you have?)
혹시	(adv.)	by any chance/I wonder
미식축구 美式蹴球	(n.)	football
좋아해요?		Do you like?
아주	(adv.)	very/so much
팬	(n.)	a fan
왜요?		Why?
이번	(adv.)	this time
토요일	(n.)	Saturday
게임	(n.)	game
~하고		together with~
좋아요		Good. Like it.
몇시		what time (시 the counter for hour)
오후 午後	(n.)	afternoon
가요 (가다)	(v.)	to go
핸드폰	(n.)	cell phone (from "hand-phone")
번호 番號	(n.)	number
제		honorific form of "my"
전화번호 電話番號	(n)	telephone number
그럼	(conn.)	then
만나요 (만나다)	(v.)	to meet

Rachel: Yoon-ho, do you have time this weekend?
Yoon-ho: Yes, I do.
Rachel: Do you like football by any chance?
Yoon-ho: Yes. I really like it. I am a fan of football. Why?
Rachel: There is a Badger game this weekend. So I'd like to go with you.
Yoon-ho: Good! What time is the game?
Rachel: It's at 2 o'clock on Saturday afternoon.
Yoon-ho: Good. Let's go together. Ah, what is your cell phone number?
Rachel: It's 987-6543. What about yours?
Yoon-ho: My phone number is 123-4567. Then see you on Saturday.

Part 2

DIALOGUE 2

Where are you now? 지금 어디예요?

Yoon-ho and Rachel meet in front of the Camp Randall stadium at 2 o'clock on Saturday afternoon, and buy tickets for a football game.

(통화 중)

윤호: 레이첼 씨, 지금 어디예요?
레이첼: 윤호 씨, 매표소 앞에 있어요.
윤호: 아, 저기 보여요. 안녕하세요!
레이첼: 아, 저도 보여요. 안녕하세요!
윤호: 자, 이제 우리 표를 사요.

(매표소에서)

윤호: 학생표 두(2) 장 주세요. 얼마예요?
직원: 오십(50) 달러예요.
윤호: 여기 있어요. 게임이 언제 시작해요?
직원: 게임은 세(3) 시에 시작해요. 그리고, 다섯(5) 시 삼십(30) 분에 끝나요.
윤호 and 레이첼: 감사합니다.

Video clip

Lesson 4: Dating 데이트하기

Word check-up

통화 通話	(n.)	a telephone call
통화 중 通話 中	(n.)	in the middle of a phone call
지금 只今	(adv.)	now/the present moment
어디예요?		Where are you?
매표소 賣票所	(n)	a ticket office
앞에	(adv.)	in front of
여기/저기	(adv.)	here/there
보여요 (보이다)	(v)	to see/to be seen
자	(adv.)	well now
이제	(adv.)	as of now/by now
표 票	(n.)	a ticket
사요 (사다)	(v.)	to buy
우리	(n.)	we
달러	(n.)	dollar
게임	(n.)	game
언제		when
시 時	(n.)	an hour/time/o'clock
시작해요 始作 (시작하다)	(v.)	to start/begin
끝나요 (끝나다)	(v.)	to end/finish
감사합니다 感謝	(v.)	thank you (a formal expression)

	(On the phone)
Yoon-ho:	Rachel, where are you now?
Rachel:	Yoon-ho, I am in front of the ticket office.
Yoon-ho:	Ah, I see you there. Hello!
Rachel:	Ah, I see you too. Hello!
Yoon-ho:	Well, let's buy the tickets now.
	(At the ticket office)
Yoon-ho:	Two student tickets, please. How much are they?
Cashier:	It's 50 dollars.
Yoon-ho:	Here it is. When does the game start?
Cashier:	The game starts at 3 o'clock, and it usually finishes around 5:30.
Yoon-ho and Rachel:	Thank you.

Part 2

Grammar and expressions

1 시간 있어요? Are you available? Do you have free time?

Koreans use the expression "시간 있어요?" (Are you available? Do you have free time?) to see if the other person is available (e.g., to talk or to do something). In general, Koreans say things indirectly because it is viewed as a polite and respectful way of making a request. Thus, instead of saying "Can you help me?" they say "Are you available/free (such that you can help me)?":

마이클: 유나 씨, **시간(이) 있어요**? Yuna, are you available/free?
유나: 왜요? Why?
마이클: 한국어 숙제 좀 도와주세요. I'd like to get help with my Korean homework.

있어요 (있다 to have) indicates the speaker possesses something (e.g., items, money), skills, or people/animals (e.g., sister, brother, cat, dog, etc.). Sometimes, learners can be confused because 있어요 is used with subject particles (~이/가), not with object particles (~을/를), although the corresponding translation in English has objects in the sentences as shown:

마이클: 저는 여자 친구**가 있어요**. (I have a girlfriend.)
유나: 저도 남자 친구**가 있어요**. (I have a boyfriend, too.)

Wait a minute: Object particles in Korean?

In this section, we will introduce another important particle, the **object particle**, in Korean. As the name indicates the object particle marks the object in the sentence. In English, some verbs require an object, which is placed right after the verb. In Korean, objects are marked by the object particle (~을/를) as shown in these examples.

- 마이클 씨는 바나나**를** 먹어요. Michael is eating a banana.
- 유나 씨는 시리얼**을** 먹어요. Yuna is eating cereal.
- 윤호 씨는 커피**를** 마셔요. Yoon-ho is drinking coffee.
- 레이첼 씨는 책**을** 읽어요. Rachel is reading a book.
- 제니퍼 씨는 친구**를** 만나요. Jennifer is meeting her friend.

Depending on the object's ending (i.e., either a consonant or a vowel ending), the variant of the object particle (을 or 를) is attached to the object nouns.

> **Variant of the object particle:**
>
> If the object ends with <u>a consonant</u>, 을 is attached. (e.g., 시리<u>얼</u>을; 책을)
> If the object ends with <u>a vowel</u>, 를 is attached. (e.g., 바나<u>나</u>를, 커<u>피</u>를, 친<u>구</u>를)

2 몇 시예요? What time is it?

What time do you get up in the morning? When does your Korean class begin? In this section, we will learn how to say the time in Korean. In Lesson 2, we've learned the Native-Korean numbers from one to five; next we introduce more Native-Korean numbers.

86

Lesson 4: Dating 데이트하기

Table 4.1 Native-Korean numbers from 1 to 12:

1	2	3	4	5	6
하나	둘	셋	넷	다섯	여섯
7	8	9	10	11	12
일곱	여덟	아홉	열	열 하나	열 둘

Now we explain how to say "the hour." For example, at 8 o'clock you get up in the morning; at 9 o'clock you eat breakfast, at 10 o'clock you have a Korean class, etc. Here are the hours of the day in Korean.

At 1 o'clock	At 2 o'clock	At 3 o'clock	At 4 o'clock	At 5 o'clock	At 6 o'clock
한 시	두 시	세 시	네 시	다섯 시	여섯 시
At 7 o'clock	At 8 o'clock	At 9 o'clock	At 10 o'clock	At 11 o'clock	At 12 o'clock
일곱 시	여덟 시	아홉 시	열 시	열한 시	열두 시

As shown, you use the *Native-Korean numbers* along with the counter for "hour" (시) and there are slight variations of the forms in numbers (i.e., 하나, 둘, 셋, 넷) when followed by the counter:

1 하나 + 시 → 한 시
2 둘 + 시 → 두 시
3 셋 + 시 → 세 시
4 넷 + 시 → 네 시

Video clip

87

Part 2

5 열 하나 (10 + 1 = 11) + 시 → 열한 시
6 열 둘 (10 + 2 = 12) + 시 → 열두 시

→ Native-Korean number + 시 (the counter for "hour")

Here are some example sentences:

마이클: 몇 시예요? What time is it?
유나: 일곱 시예요. It is 7 o'clock.
수지: 지금 몇 시예요? What time is it now? (지금 now)
탐: 지금은 열한 시예요. It is 11 o'clock now.

[Practice 1]

Answer the question "지금 몇 시예요?" using the clues given.

1 It is 9 o'clock →
2 It is 12 o'clock →
3 It is 3 o'clock →

Before we talk more about "how to say the minutes," we'll introduce the Sino-Korean numbers from 1 to 60 in the following table.

1	2	3	4	5	6	7	8	9	10
일	이	삼	사	오	육	칠	팔	구	십
11	12	13	14	15	16	17	18	19	20
십일	십이	십삼	십사	십오	십육	십칠	십팔	십구	이십
21	22	23	24	25	26	27	28	29	30
이십 일	이십 이	이십 삼	이십 사	이십 오	이십 육	이십 칠	이십 팔	이십 구	삼십
31	32	33	34	35	36	37	38	39	40
삼십	삼십 일	삼십 삼	삼십 사	삼십 오	삼십 육	삼십 칠	삼십 팔	삼실 구	사십
41	42	43	44	45	46	47	48	49	50
사십	사십 일	사십 삼	사십 사	사십 오	사십 육	사십 칠	사십 팔	사십 구	오십
51	52	53	54	55	56	57	58	59	60
오십	오십 일	오십 삼	오십 사	오십 오	오십 육	오십 칠	오십 팔	오십 구	육십

Sino-Korean numbers are:

10 = 십 (not '일십' but just '십')
11 = 10 + 1 (십일)
12 = 10 + 2 (십이)
13 = 10 + 3 (십삼)
20 = 2 × 10 (이십)
21 = 2 × 10 + 1 (이십 일)
22 = 2 × 10 + 2 (이십 이)
30 = 3 × 10 (삼십)
31 = 3 × 10 + 1 (삼십 일)

Lesson 4: Dating 데이트하기

You are now ready to say the hours and minutes in Korean. Here are some examples:

1 It is 3:15. → 세 시 십오 분이에요. (십오 분=십오 15 + 분 minute)
2 It is 4:27. → 네 시 이십 칠 분이에요. (이십 칠 분=이십 칠 27 + 분 minute)
3 It is 9:09. → 아홉 시 구 분이에요.

How do we say the hours and minutes in Korean?

Hour	Minute
Native-Korean number + 시 (the counter for "hour") 한 시, 두 시, 세 시, 네 시, 다섯 시, 여섯 시, 일곱 시, 여덟 시, 아홉 시, 열 시; 열한 시, 열두 시	Sino-Korean number + 분 (the counter for "minute") 오 분, 십 분, 십오 분, 이십 분, 삼십 분, 사십 분, 오십 분, 오십 오 분

[Practice 2]

Using the times given next, answer the question "지금 몇 시예요?" in Korean.

1 It is 11:45. →
2 It is 2:30. →
3 It is 7:05. →

How can we tell "It is 8 am" from "It is 8 pm" in Korean? Now that you know how to say the time in Korean, you might still be wondering how to distinguish am from pm in telling time in Korean. Here is the answer for you.

am: before noon	pm: after noon
오전 오전 8 (여덟) 시예요. It is 8 am.	오후 오후 8 (여덟) 시예요. It is 8 pm.

[Practice 3]

Answer the question "지금 몇 시예요?" in Korean.

1 It is 3:15 pm. →
2 It is 6: 30 am. →
3 It is 10:30 pm. →

At 8:30 여덟 시 삼십 분 and 여덟 시 반?

There are two ways to say "8:30." So far we've learned that we say '여덟 시 삼십 분' for "It is 8:30," and you may hear Koreans also say '여덟 시 반' for the same time as shown in the example.

지금 몇 시예요? What time is it now?
→ 여덟 시 삼십 분이에요. ✔
→ 여덟 시 반이에요. ✔

'반' means "half" and '여덟 시 반' means it is half an hour after 8 o'clock. So you can use these two time expressions for 8:30 from now on.

89

Part 2

3 게임이 몇 시에 있어요? What time is the game?

You want to know when the game starts, so you ask "게임이 몇 시에 있어요?" In response, your classmate answers by saying '[time]+에 있어요':

You:	미식축구 게임이 *몇 시에* 있어요? What time is the football game?
Your classmate:	두 시에 있어요. It is at 2 o'clock.
다미:	한국어 수업이 *몇 시에* 있어요? When is your Korean class?
마이클:	한 시 오 분에 있어요. It is at 1:05 pm.
	→ [time: ___시 or ___시 ___분] 에 있어요:

You may notice that the time expression is followed by the particle '~에'. In Lesson 2, with the verb '가다' (to go) we learned the destination is marked with the destination particle ~에, as in 마이클 씨는 도서관에 가요; 저는 학교에 가요. Here, the particle '~에' is also used to mark the time; in this context it is called the "time particle."

[Practice]

Answer the question "한국어 수업이 몇 시에 있어요?"

1 at 3:30 pm →
2 at 10:05 am →
3 at 1:20 pm →

4 윤호 씨하고 같이 가고 싶어요. I want to go with Yoon-ho.

There are many things you probably like to do with another person, such as go to the movie theater, play tennis, or play a video game. In the dialogue in this lesson, Rachel wanted to go to a Korean grocery with Yoon-ho as shown:

사라: 윤호 씨하고 같이 한국 마트에 가고 싶어요. (한국 마트 Korean grocery)
윤호: 미안해요. 다른 약속이 있어요. (다른 other; 약속 appointment)

The expression [noun] + 하고/같이 is used for expressing "doing things together." 같이 "together" can be omitted without changing the meaning. It should also be noted that the word '같이' is pronounced [가치].

마이클 씨하고 *같이* 영화를 보고 싶어요 (= 마이클 씨하고 영화를 보고 싶어요).
유나 씨하고 *같이* 테니스를 치고 싶어요 (= 유나 씨하고 테니스를 치고 싶어요).

If you are not comfortable with the structure ~고 싶어요, go back and review Lesson 3.

[Practice]

Answer the following questions in Korean using ~하고 같이.

1 누구하고 같이 저녁을 먹고 싶어요? (누구하고 with whom)
2 누구하고 같이 영화를 보고 싶어요?
3 보통 누구하고 같이 공부를 해요? (보통 usually, in general)
4 누구하고 같이 여행을 하고 싶어요? (여행 travel)

Lesson 4: Dating 데이트하기

5 제 전화번호는 123-4567.이에요. My phone number is 123-4567.

One of your Korean friends asks you for your phone number so you can get together over the weekend; you want to tell him/her your phone number in Korean. This section will help you with that.

마이클: 유나 씨, 전화번호(가) 뭐예요?
유나: 제 전화번호요? 왜요?
마이클: 주말에 유나 씨하고 같이 영화(를) 보고 싶어요.
유나: 네, 제 전화번호는 123–4567 [일이삼에 사오육칠] 이에요.

Video clip

Here is how to read the phone numbers in Korean:

333–4567 → 삼삼삼에 사오육칠이에요.
509–9602 → 오공팔에 구육공이예요. (The zero in Korean is either 공 or 영.)

As shown, the first three digits are followed by ~에 in Korean (as in 삼삼삼에 333-. . .).

[Practice 1]

Say the following phone numbers in Korean.

1 278-4592 →
2 608-2017 →
3 419-7603 →

91

Part 2

[Practice 2]

Ask for your classmates' cell numbers, and write down the numbers.

You will ask "핸드폰 번호가 뭐예요?"

1 Classmate 1's cell number →
2 Classmate 2's cell number →
3 Classmate 3's cell number →

6 지금 어디예요? Where are you now?

The expression "지금 어디예요?" is frequently used to ask about the whereabouts of the other person on the phone. Here is a sample dialogue:

민지: 여보세요. 마이클 씨, 지금 어디예요?
마이클: 도서관이에요. 민지 씨는 지금 어디예요?
민지: 저는 스타벅스에 있어요.

Hello? 여보세요?

The expression "여보세요" is typically used to initiate conversations on the phone. When you make a call, the other party answers the phone by saying "여보세요" (hello). In some cases, when you want to get someone's attention and yet that person is not on the scene (e.g., you are visiting someone's place, and knocking on the door, but nobody answers the door), you may use this expression 여보세요 in order to grab someone's attention.

[Practice]

Make a phone call to one of your Korean friends, and ask about where she/he is now with the question "지금 어디예요?"

7 얼마예요? How much is it?/여기 있어요. Here it is

If you are a coffee lover, you probably would enjoy a cup of hot cappuccino every morning. The good news is that you can now order coffee using Korean. Next time you are at a Starbucks in Korea, you can use the following conversation to order your coffee.

마이클: 카푸치노 주세요. 얼마예요?
종업원: 사천 원이에요. (사천 원 4,000원 won 3.5 달러 dollars)
마이클: 여기 있어요.
종업원: 여기 카푸치노 있어요.
마이클: 감사합니다.

[Role play 1]

At a pizza restaurant in Korea, you can order a pepperoni pizza using Korean.

You: 페퍼로니 피자 주세요. 얼마예요? (페퍼로니 피자 pepperoni pizza)
종업원: 6달러 99센트예요 (육 달러 구십 구 센트)
You: 여기 있어요.

Lesson 4: Dating 데이트하기

종업원: 감사합니다. 여기 페퍼로니 피자 있어요.
YOU: 감사합니다.

[Role play 2]

At a McDonald's in Korea, you can order a meal using Korean.

You: 불고기 햄버거 하나 주세요. 그리고 콜라도 하나 주세요. 얼마예요?
종업원: 5달러 99센트예요. (오 달러 구십 구 센트)
You: 여기 있어요.
종업원: 감사합니다. 여기 불고기 햄버거 있어요. 콜라도 있어요.
You: 감사합니다.

Part 2

Activity 1

My dating plan 1

주말에 친구와 데이트를 하고 싶어요. You want to go on a date with your friend.
누구와 데이트하고 싶어요? Who would you like to go on a date with?
그 친구에게 전화로 데이트 신청을 해 보세요. Make a call to your friend, and ask for a date.

친구이름 Your partner		Answers
전화번호	telephone number	
주말에시간이있어요?	Do you have time this weekend?	
언제시간이있어요?	When do you have time?	
뭐하고싶어요?	What do you want to do?	
어디에서만나고싶어요?	Where do you want to meet?	

Making a phone call for date plans
Pixabay.com

Lesson 4: Dating 데이트하기

Activity 2

My dating plan 2

다음의 데이트 장소를 보고, 두 명의 티켓을 사 보세요.
Let's buy tickets for you and your date for the following places.

야구 경기장 Baseball stadium
Pixabay.com

영화관 Movie theater
Pixabay.com

미식축구 American football
Pixabay.com

95

Part 2

Conversation

You: 우리 영화를 봐요! Let's watch a movie!
영화 표 두 장 주세요. Give me two tickets for the movie.
얼마예요? How much is it?
매표소: 30 달러 예요. It's 30 dollars.
You: 여기 있어요. Here it is. 영화가 언제 시작해요? When does the movie start?
매표소: 영화가 다섯 시에 시작해요. The movie starts at 5pm.
그리고 여섯 시 삼십 분에 끝나요. And it will be over by 6:30pm.
You: 감사합니다. Thank you.

Cultural notes

Korean currency, "won"

Korea's official monetary unit is the "won." It is indicated by KRW or W with bars through it. You will also see "won" written after the amount. Korean currency comes in coins and bills. The Korean government recently released a new design for small-size bills that includes pictures of renowned Korean figures and culture. Exchange rates vary, but $1 US is roughly 1125.26 won nowadays. Most of the businesses in Korea widely use and accept payment by credit card. When you need to exchange your foreign currency into Korean won, visit a bank or currency exchange service center. If you travel to Korea, you can exchange your money into the local currency at bank branches located in the airport.

Korean won banknotes, Cheon Won, O-Cheon Won, Man Won, O-Man Won
Photograph provided by authors

1,000원	5,000원	10,000원	50,000원
천 원(Cheon Won)	오천 원(O-Cheon Won)	만 원(Man Won)	오만 원(O-Man Won)

Korea–Yonsei varsity games

To kick off the school year, Korea–Yonsei varsity games called Ko-Yon-Jeon (고연전) are held. These spectacular inter-varsity rivalry sports matches between Korea University (Ko) and Yonsei University (Yon) include 야구 baseball, 농구 basketball, 아이스하키 ice hockey, 럭비 rugby, and 축구 soccer. The matches are held in a huge stadium in Seoul not belonging to either university in order to make the games fair. During Ko-Yon-Jeon, there are two nights of partying and drinking in Sinchon and Anam, where the universities are located. In the stadium, thousands of college students and alums dance, sing, cheer, and jeer as cheerleaders get dressed up. Each varsity team has "cheer training" a few days before the games: Students from each university gather to learn special cheers and dances to popular K-pop songs to intimidate the other team and also to entertain the fans.

Lesson 4: Dating 데이트하기

Vocabulary expansion

밑줄 친 단어를 보세요. 상자 안에 있는 단어를 사용해서 다음의 대화를 연습하세요. Please look at the underlined words. Use the words in the box to practice the following conversations.

Let's learn some vocabulary related to sports

나는 <u>미식축구</u>를 좋아해요. 그래서 친구하고 같이 <u>경기장</u> 에 자주 가요. 미식축구 선수는 공을 멀리 <u>던져요</u>. 제일 좋아하는 <u>미식축구</u> <u>선수</u>는 애론 로져스예요.

[Translation]

I like American football. That's why I regularly go to the stadium with my friends. Football players throw the ball far. My favorite football player is Aaron Rodgers.

Vocabulary

치어리더	cheer leader
응원하다	to cheer, shout for
응원가	a fight song
마스코트	a mascot
씨름	Korean traditional wrestling
씨름판	wresting ring
샅바를 잡아요 (잡다)	thigh hold
골프	golf
필드	field
공을 쳐요 (치다)	hit a ball
미식축구	American football
경기장	stadium
공	ball
던져요 (던지다)	throw (a ball)

골프 golf
Pixabay.com

씨름 Korean traditional wrestling
Pixabay.com

Part 3

Contents

5 Weather and health 날씨와 건강

6 Thanksgiving Day and Chuseok 추수감사절과 추석

7 Korean market and college clubs/student organizations 한인 마트와 대학 동아리

8 Studying Korean 한국어 공부하기

Lesson 5

Weather and health
날씨와 건강

Learning goals

- Past-tense forms
- Basic expressions of weather and health

Grammar and expressions

- 흐려요. Adjectives (or descriptive verbs)
- 날씨가 참 좋네요. Sentence ending ~네요
- 공부 많이 했어요? making a verb past-tense
- 안 했어요 vs. 못 했어요. Negative adverbs
- 윤호 씨는요? 김 선생님은요? Noun + 는/은요?
- 목도 아프고 열도 있어요. ~and ~and

Activities

- Let's talk about the weather around the world
- Writing a letter

Part 3

Cultural notes

- Korean home remedies
- How to say "thank you" in Korean

Vocabulary expansion

- Words to use in hospitals

Lesson 5: Weather and health 날씨와 건강

DIALOGUE 1

Today's weather is so nice. 날씨가 참 좋아요

Yoon-ho and Rachel talk about the weather, and ask each other about studying for midterms.

윤호: 레이첼 씨, 안녕하세요? 오늘 날씨가 참 좋아요.
레이첼: 아, 안녕하세요, 윤호 씨. 그러게요. 오늘 날씨가 아주 좋네요.
윤호: 참, 레이첼 씨, 한국어 시험 공부는 많이 했어요?
레이첼: 아니요, 많이 못 했어요. 윤호 씨는요?
윤호: 저는 많이 했어요.
레이첼: 그래요? 그럼 좀 가르쳐주세요.
 (공부 후)
윤호: 레이첼 씨, 날씨가 흐려요!
레이첼: 맞아요. 비가 와요. 윤호 씨, 우산 있어요?
윤호: 아니요, 없어요. 레이첼 씨는요?
레이첼: 저도 없어요.

Video clip

103

Part 3

Word check-up

오늘	(n.)	today
날씨	(n.)	weather
참	(affix)	very
그러게요		Yes/I suppose.
좋네요 (좋다)	(it is)	good
시험 試驗	(n.)	exam/test
공부 工夫	(n.)	study
많이	(adj.)	a lot
못	(adv.)	can not
했어요 (했다)	(v.)	did
~는요?		What about~?
저는		honorific form of I
좀		abbreviated form of 조금
가르쳐요 (가르치다)	(v.)	to teach
흐려요 (흐리다)	(adj.)	to be cloudy
비가 와요 (비가 오다)	(v.)	to rain
우산 雨傘	(n.)	umbrella
저도		me as well
없어요 (없다)	(v.)	there is not/do not have

DIALOGUE 2

I don't feel well. 몸이 좀 안 좋아요

Yoon-ho calls Rachel to check up on her. She did not come to school because she's sick.

윤호:	여보세요? 레이첼 씨, 저 윤호예요.
레이첼:	윤호 씨 . . .
윤호:	오늘 학교에 왜 안 왔어요?
레이첼:	몸이 좀 안 좋아요.
윤호:	그래요? 많이 아파요?
레이첼:	목이 아프고 열도 좀 있어요.
윤호:	기침도 해요?
레이첼:	아니요. 기침은 안 해요.
윤호:	약은 먹었어요?
레이첼:	네, 아침에 감기약을 먹었어요.
윤호:	그럼, 물도 많이 마시고 푹 쉬어요.
레이첼:	고마워요.

Video clip

Part 3

Word check-up

여보세요?		Hello? (on the phone)
오늘	(n.)	today
왜	(adv.)	why
학교 學校	(n.)	school
안	(adv.)	not
왔어요?		Did you come?
몸	(n.)	body
많이	(adv.)	very/so
아파요 (아프다)	(adj.)	to be sick
목	(n.)	neck
열 熱	(n.)	fever
~도		too/also/as well
기침	(n.)	cough
약 藥	(n.)	medicine
감기약 感氣藥	(n.)	cold medicine
물	(n.)	water
푹	(adv.)	enough/completely
쉬어요 (쉬다)	(v.)	to rest
고마워요		Thank you

Grammar and expressions

1 흐려요. Adjectives (or descriptive verbs)

This section introduces the most frequently used descriptive verbs (or adjectives) in Korean along with their conjugated forms. Here are the descriptive verbs you should know.

Basic form: Stem – ending	Meaning	Conjugated form (in present tense)
예쁘 – 다	to be beautiful, pretty	예뻐요
크 – 다	to be big	커요
작 – 다	to be small	작아요
많 – 다	to be plenty	많아요
적 – 다	to be lacking	적어요
친절하 – 다	to be kind	친절해요
깨끗하 – 다	to be clean	깨끗해요
좋 – 다	to be nice, good	좋아요

Lesson 5: Weather and health 날씨와 건강

Basic form: Stem – ending	Meaning	Conjugated form (in present tense)
나쁘 – 다	to be bad	나빠요
멋있 – 다	to be attractive, cool	멋있어요
귀엽 – 다	to be cute	귀여워요
아프 – 다	to be sick, ill	아파요
춥 – 다	to be cold	추워요
덥 – 다	to be warm	더워요
흐리 – 다	to be cloudy	흐려요

[Practice]

Using the descriptive verbs, talk about your classmates. Here are sample sentences: 마이클 씨는 키가 커요. 안나 씨는 예뻐요.

Now it is your turn. If you need more descriptive verbs, ask your instructor.

1 _____ .
2 _____ .
3 _____ .

Let's review conjugation rules! Repeat from Lesson 2

- If the stem ends with the vowel 아 or 오 , add the ending ~아요:
일어나 + 아요→ 일어<u>나아</u> 요 (vowel contraction) → 일어나요
- If the stem ends with the vowel other than (아 or 오), add the ending ~어요: 먹 + 어요→ 먹어요
- If the stem ends with ~하, add the ending ~여요, and then further contract it into 해요:
공부하 + → 공부하 + 여요 → 공부 (하 + 여 요→ 해요) → 공부해요
- If the stem ends with a vowel ~으, delete the vowel — and add ~어요:
쓰~ + → ㅆ + 어요→ 써요

2 날씨가 참 좋네요. Sentence ending ~네요

What is the difference between the two sentences?

1 날씨가 좋아요.
2 날씨가 좋네요.

As shown, the two sentences are identical except for the sentencing endings: 좋-아요 vs. 좋-네요. The simple translation for both sentences can be "The weather is good." However, the second sentence uses (Korean '~네요'), which provides additional information. The ending ~네요 reveals the speaker's immediate realization of his/her subjective emotion (such as amazement, surprise, or astonishment) regarding the given fact. The first sentence, "날씨가 좋아요," simply describes the good weather, while the second sentence, "날씨가 좋네요," shows that the speaker is amazed or surprised by the weather. Thus, an intended reading of sentence (2) can be "I am amazed at the good weather, which is unseasonably *good*."

107

Part 3

[Practice]

Tell us the difference between the following two sentences.

1 마이클 씨 여자 친구가 예뻐요. vs. 마이클 씨의 여자 친구가 예쁘네요.
2 여기 불고기가 맛있어요. vs. 여기 불고기가 맛있네요.

3 공부 많이 했어요? Making a verb past tense

"What did you do last night?" In comparison to how we express our thoughts at the present moment, this section introduces how to say or describe things in the past in Korean. To show you the difference in form between the two tenses, we will repeat the verbs used in Lesson 2.

Basic form: stem – ending	Meaning	Conjugated form (in present tense)	Conjugated form (in past tense)
일어나 – 다	to wake up	일어나요	일어났어요
먹 – 다	to eat	먹어요	먹었어요
공부하 – 다	to study	공부해요	공부했어요
자 – 다	to sleep	자요	잤어요
쓰 – 다	to write	써요	썼어요

Making a verb past-tense in Korean:

Step 1: drop the ending ~요 from the congugated form in present tense (e.g., 가요 → 가 ~) → **Step 2**: add ~ㅆ어요 to the remaining form (e.g., 가 + ㅆ어요) → **Step 3**: Combine them together for the past-tensed form (e.g., 갔어요).

1 일어나-요 → 일어나 + ~ㅆ어요→ 일어났어요
2 먹어-요 → 먹어 + ~ㅆ어요 → 먹었어요
3 공부해-요 → 공부해 + ~ㅆ어요 → 공부했어요
4 자-요 → 자 + ~ㅆ어요 → 잤어요
5 써-요 → 써 + ~ㅆ어요 → 썼어요

[Practice]

Let's practice more with other verbs.

Basic form: stem – ending	Meaning	Conjugated form in present tense	Drop ~요 + add ~ㅆ 어요	Conjugated form in past tense
(e.g.,) 읽다	to read	읽어요	읽어~ + ㅆ 어요	읽었어요
가 – 다	to go	가요		
오 – 다	to come	와요		
청소하 – 다	to clean, organize	청소해요		
테니스를 치 – 다	to play tennis	테니스를 쳐요		

108

Lesson 5: Weather and health 날씨와 건강

Pronunciation 맞아요 → [마자요]

맞아요 → [마자요]. For pronunciation, the syllable-final consonant (here 'ㅈ' in '맞') is carried over to the next syllable when it is followed by any vowel (in this case '아요'). Thus it is pronounced 마-자-요. Square brackets indicate pronunciation in the following examples.

있어요 → [이써요]; 앉아요 → [안자요]; 먹어요 → [머거요]; 읽어요 → [일거요]

4 안 했어요. vs. 못 했어요 negative adverbs

We often find ourselves in a situation where we can't tell whether "We <u>don't</u> do it" or "we <u>can't</u> do it." The distinction between "Don't do it" and "Can't do it" can be blurred, and yet we usually distinguish correctly depending upon the speaker's control over the situations in question. Here are examples of using these two negative adverbs along with the given contexts.

● (Context: 어제 아팠어요.) 그래서 숙제를 <u>못</u> 했어요. I couldn't do my homework.
● (Context: 수학 수업이 재미없었어요.) 그래서 숙제를 <u>안</u> 했어요. I didn't do my homework.

As shown, you *couldn't* do your homework assignment because you were sick yesterday, while you *didn't* do your homework because the subject does not interest you at all. Here are more examples:

● 오늘은 바빠서 친구 파티에 <u>못</u> 가요. I can't go . . . because . . .
● 친구하고 싸워서 친구 파티에 <u>안</u> 가요. I don't go . . . because . . .

You *can't* go to the party tonight because you are busy, whereas you *don't want to* go to the party because you had an argument with your friend who was hosting the party.

Here are tips for locating these negative adverbs within sentences.

● 저는 책을 읽어요. → 저는 책을 안/못 읽어요.
 → Put 안/못 between the object and the verb.

● 방이 깨끗해요. → 방이 <u>안</u> 깨끗해요.
 → Put 안 before the descriptive verb.

5 윤호 씨는요? 김 선생님은요? Noun + 는/은요?

This is a typical conversation between two friends.

안나: 마이클 씨, 안녕하세요? <u>오늘 기분이 어때요?</u>
마이클: 아주 좋아요. 안나 씨는 <u>오늘 기분이 어때요?</u>
안나: 저도 좋아요.

As shown, the expression "오늘 기분이 어때요?" (How are you feeling today?) is repeated. In the authentic conversation, people often shorten the conversation replacing "오늘 기분이 어때요?" with '~는/은요?' as shown.

안나: 마이클 씨, 안녕하세요? 오늘 기분이 어때요?
마이클: 아주 좋아요. 안나 씨<u>는요</u>? (sentence shortened to avoid repetition)
안나: 저도 좋아요.

109

Part 3

Instead of repeating the same part in the conversation, you can shorten it using '~는/은요?' in colloquial conversation. The variation '~는/은 + 요' depends on the previous noun form.

● If the noun/word ends with <u>a consonant</u> (e.g., 마이클) → then, "마이클은요?"
● If the noun/word ends with <u>a vowel</u> (e.g., 마이클 <u>씨</u>) → then, "마이클 씨는요?"

[Practice]

Use the following dialogues to role play with your classmates.

마이클: 제인 씨, 오늘 시간이 있어요?
제인: 미안해요. 오늘은 아주 바빠요?
마이클: 그럼, 내일은요? (내일 tomorrow)
제인: 내일도 시간이 없어요.
마이클: 그럼, 모레는요? (모레 the day after tomorrow)
제인: _____ .

6 목도 아프고 열도 있어요. ~and ~and

In Lesson 3, we learned the sentence connective 그리고 ("*And*") as shown:

● 린다는 커피를 좋아해요. <u>그리고</u> 린다는 레몬차도 좋아해요.

We can rewrite this using ~고 without any difference in meaning. In addition, you can also add ~도.

● 린다는 커피를 좋아하<u>고</u> 레몬차<u>도</u> 좋아해요.
● 린다는 커피를 좋아하<u>고</u> , 레몬차<u>도</u> 좋아하<u>고</u> , 인삼차<u>도</u> 좋아하<u>고</u> , 녹차<u>도</u> 좋아해요.

(레몬차 lemon tea; 인삼차 ginseng tea; 녹차 green tea)

Using ~고, you can add two or more sentences with different subjects, too.

● 린다는 커피를 좋아해요. 그리고 마이클은 녹차를 좋아해요.
● <u>린다는</u> 커피를 좋아하고 <u>마이클은</u> 녹차를 좋아해요.

[Practice]

Ask your classmates about their favorite tea and report their answers back to your classmates using ~고.

Sample sentences: 마이클은 커피를 좋아하<u>고</u> 제니퍼는 콜라를 좋아하<u>고</u> 링링은 오렌지 주스를 좋아해요.

1 _____ .
2 _____ .
3 _____ .
4 _____ .
5 _____ .

There are expressions that sound very similar, yet have very different meanings

배가 *아파*요. I have a stomachache.
배가 *고파*요. I am hungry.

110

고향이 어디예요? Where is your *hometown*?
고양이가 어디에 있어요? Where is the *cat*?
공항이 어디예요? Where is the *airport*?

Exercises

● Using the negative adverb **안**, re-write the following sentences as negative sentences.
  1 마이클 씨는 키가 커요. →
  2 제니퍼 씨의 방은 깨끗해요. →
  3 앤디 씨는 친절해요. →
  4 머리가 아파요. →
  5 민지 씨는 귀여워요. →

● Answer the following questions in Korean.
  6 어제 오후 7시에 뭐 했어요?
  7 지난주 일요일에 어디에 갔어요?
  8 오늘 아침에 뭐 먹었어요?
  9 어제 스타벅스에서 누구를 만났어요?
  10 오늘 기분이 어때요?

● Complete the following conversation with the choices given.
  [배가 아파요; 배가 고파요; 그럼; 그리고; 그런데; 그래서; 알아요; 몰라요]

  제니퍼: 어디에 가요?
  토마스: 지금 (11) _____ . (12) _____ , 한국 식당에 가요.
  제니퍼: 식당이 어디에 있어요?
  토마스: 스테이트 스트리트 (State St.) (13) _____ ?
  제니퍼: 네.
  토마스: 스테이트 스트리트에 있어요.

● Write the pronunciation forms as shown in the example.
  [Example] 문앞에→ [무나페]
  14 작아요 → [   ]
  15 많아요 → [   ]
  16 멋있어요 → [   ]
  17 일어나요 → [   ]

Part 3

Activity 1

Let's talk about the weather around the world

오늘 세계 날씨가 어때요? What is the weather like in other countries now? 세계의 여러나라와 여러분 나라의 날씨를 반 친구들과 이야기해봅시다. Let's talk about the weather in the world and in your hometown.
다음 활동지에 날씨를 써 보세요. Fill out the weather in the table that follows.

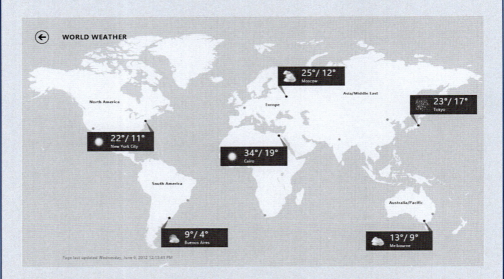

World weather
Image created by authors

나라 Country	도시 City	표현 Expression	오늘 날씨가 어때요?
러시아 Russia	모스크바 Moscow	날씨가 좋다	러시아 모스크바(은)/는 날씨가 좋아요.
일본 Japan	도쿄 Tokyo	비가 오다	
호주 Australia	멜버른 Melbourne	흐리다	
이집트 Egypt	카이로 Cairo	바람이 불다	
아르헨티나 Argentina	부에노스 아이레스 Buenos Aires	춥다	
미국 United States	뉴욕 New York	눈이 오다	

Lesson 5: Weather and health 날씨와 건강

Activity 2

Writing a letter

린다가 몸이 안 좋아요. 목이 아프고 열도 좀 있어요. 다음의 표현을 활용해서 린다에게 이메일을 보내 주세요. Linda has been sick for more than two weeks. She has a sore throat and fever. Using the expressions provided, let's write an email to ask if she is all right.

A note for writing a letter to Linda
Image created by authors

Email to send a letter to Linda
Pixabay.com

Vocabulary list that you can use for your letter

아프다	sick
목	throat
통증	pain
열	fever
약	medicine
병원	hospital
춥다	(feel) cold
괜찮아요?	Are you okay?

113

Part 3

Cultural notes

Korean home remedies

Are you feeling under the weather? In Korea, there are many restorative and medicinal foods to boost your well-being. Korean people believe food and medicine have always been closely related. Here are some Korean home remedies for colds, sore throats, hangovers, and low energy.

1   *Seol-reong-tang* 설렁탕: This is made by simmering the bones, head, and meat of an ox for approximately six to seven hours. 설렁탕contains amino acids and calcium; it helps energize your body and aid digestion. The collagen in설렁탕 is good for your bones and skin.
2   *Yu-ja-cha* 유자차: The fruit called yu-ja 유자 is packed with vitamin C. Thinly slice yu-ja and combine it with honey, then preserve it in jars. If you feel tired and have a cold, head-ache, or sore throat, put some preserved yu-ja into a cup, add hot water, and enjoy 유자차 (차 means "tea").
3   *Sam-gye-tang* 삼계탕: This is a kind of chicken soup made with ginseng. Korean people used to eat this during the summer months in an effort to fight the heat (of summer) with the heat (of the soup). When you sweat a lot in summer, try 삼계탕 that has ginseng and other stamina-enhancing ingredients such as jujube, ginkgo nut, and garlic.
4   *Kong-na-mul-guk* 콩나물국: Korean bean sprout soup, 콩나물국, is a cheap and easy way to fight hangovers. Bean sprouts are full of vitamin C and a special chemical called aspara-gine that may help people control hangovers.

How to say "Thank you" in Korean

It is important for Korean language learners to know when and how to say "Thank you" in Korean. There are several ways of saying "Thank you" depending on the relationship between the speakers and the level of respect that needs to be conveyed. 감사합니다 is the most formal way of saying "Thank you." It is respectful and commonly heard. 감사합니다 should be used toward elders, bosses, and strangers in a formal situation. 고맙습니다 is also respectful. Although it isn't used quite as frequently as 감사합니다, it is still very common. 고마워요 is a simple and yet still polite way of saying "Thank you." The casual form, 고마워, should be used only with people you have known for a while and are comfortable with (e.g., friends, classmates).

Vocabulary expansion

상자 안에 있는 단어를 사용해서 다음의 대화를 연습하세요. Use the words in the box to prac-tice the following conversations.

여러분이 배가 아파서 병원에 가요

아래 세 장소에서 무엇을 해야 할까요? 다음의 단어를 사용해서 순서대로 설명해보세요. You may have to see a doctor at a hospital because you have a pain in your belly. What would you need to do in the following situations? Explain the situations in detail using the vocabulary provided.

114

Lesson 5: Weather and health 날씨와 건강

Vocabulary

접수하다	to register
간호사	a nurse
기다리다	to wait
안내하다	to guide/to inform

구급차 ambulance
Pixabay.com

약	medicine
따뜻한 차	warm tea
먹다	to eat/take
쉬다	to take rests
자다	to sleep

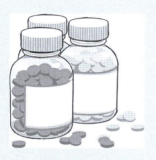

약 medicine
Pixabay.com

의사	a doctor
청진기	stethoscope
진찰하다	to examine
주사맞다	to get a shot

의사 doctor
Pixabay.com

115

Part 3

Translations of Dialogues I and II

Dialogue 1

Yoon-ho: Rachel, hello? Today's weather is so good.
Rachel: Ah, hello Yoon-ho. Yes, I suppose. Today's weather is very good.
Yoon-ho: By the way, Rachel, did you study a lot for the Korean exam?
Rachel: No, I did not. What about you, Yoon-ho?
Yoon-ho: I studied a lot.
Rachel: Really? Then please help me.

(after studying)

Yoon-ho: Rachel, the weather is cloudy.
Rachel: You're right. It's raining. Do you have an umbrella, Yoon-ho?
Yoon-ho: No, I do not. What about you, Rachel?
Rachel: I do not have one either.

Dialogue 2

(on the phone)

Yoon-ho: Hello? Rachel, it's Yoon-ho.
Rachel: Yoon-ho . . .
Yoon-ho: Why didn't you come to school today?
Rachel: I don't feel good.
Yoon-ho: Really? Are you very sick?
Rachel: My throat hurts and I have a fever.
Yoon-ho: Do you have a cough as well?
Rachel: No. I don't have a cough.
Yoon-ho: Did you take some medicine?
Rachel: Yes, I took some cold medicine this morning.
Yoon-ho: Then, drink a lot of water and get enough rest.
Rachel: Thank you.

Lesson 6

Thanksgiving Day and Chuseok
추수감사절과 추석

Learning goals

- Make inquiries about words/expressions.
- Describe things, people, and animals.
- Make suggestions.

Grammar and expressions

- 무슨 음식? What kind of food?
- 한국어로 ___ (이/가) 뭐예요? How do you say ___ in Korean?/ ~(이)라고 해요. It is said ~ in Korean.
- 불고기하고 떡볶이. A and B
- 추석(이) 언제예요? When is Chuseok?
- 추석에 뭐 했어요? What did you do on Chuseok?
- 반달처럼 생겼어요. It is shaped like a crescent moon.
- 떡볶이를 만들어서 친구하고 같이 먹었어요: ~어서/아서. Two events sequentially connected.
- 윷놀이 게임을 해 볼까요? Shall we play a game?

Activities

- Role play: Thanksgiving Day
- Let's play Yut

117

Part 3

Cultural notes

- When is Chuseok?
- On your way home for Chuseok

Vocabulary expansion

- Words for holidays

118

Lesson 6: Thanksgiving Day and Chuseok 추수감사절과 추석

DIALOGUE 1

Coming back from Thanksgiving.
다녀왔어요

Rachel came back to school after visiting her hometown for Thanksgiving. Yoon-ho and Rachel talk about Thanksgiving in the United States.

윤호: 레이첼 씨, Thanksgiving Day 에 뭐 했어요?

레이첼: 시카고 집에 다녀왔어요.

윤호: 추수감사절에는 보통 무슨 음식을 먹어요?

레이첼: **추-수-감-사-절?** 추수감사절이 뭐예요?

윤호: 아, Thanksgiving Day 를 한국어로 추-수-감-사-절이라고 해요.

레이첼: 아, 그래요. 그럼, turkey는 한국어로 뭐예요?

윤호: Turkey는 한국어로 **칠-면-조**예요.

레이첼: 칠-면-조. 네, 추수감사절에는 보통 칠면조 고기하고 파이를 먹어요. 이번 추수감사절에도 칠면조 고기하고 호박 파이를 많이 먹었어요. 아주 맛있었어요.

윤호: 그리고? 뭐 했어요?

레이첼: 추수감사절에는 세일을 크게 해요. 그래서 가족들과 함께 저녁을 먹고 백화점에서 쇼핑을 했어요. 큰 텔레비전도 하나 샀어요.

Video clip

119

Part 3

Word check-up

시카고	(n.)	Chicago
집	(n.)	home/house
다녀왔어요 (다녀오다)	(v.)	to go and come back (past tense)
추수감사절 秋收感恩節	(n.)	Thanksgiving Day
보통	(adv.)	in general/ usually
먹어요 (먹다)	(v.)	to eat
한국어로 韓國語-		in Korean
~(이)라고 해요	(something)	is called~
칠면조 七面鳥	(n.)	turkey
칠면조 고기	(n.)	turkey meat
호박 파이	(n.)	pumpkin pie
세일	(n.)	sale; 세일을 하다 (v.) to be on sale
세일을 크게 하다		to have a huge sale
가족들 家族	(n.)	family members (cf. ~들 plural markers in Korean)
큰	(adj.)	big, huge
백화점 百貨店	(n.)	department store
쇼핑했어요 (쇼핑하다)	(v.)	to shop (past tense)
큰 (크다)	(adj.)	big/huge
텔레비전	(n.)	television
하나	(numb.)	one (thing)
샀어요 (사다)	(v.)	to buy (past tense)

Lesson 6: Thanksgiving Day and Chuseok 추수감사절과 추석

DIALOGUE 2

Shall we? 해 볼까요?

Rachel asks Yoon-ho whether Korea has a traditional holiday like Thanksgiving. In response, Yoon-ho talks to Rachel about Chuseok.

레이첼: 그런데, 윤호 씨는 추수감사절에 뭐 했어요?

윤호: 친구하고 같이 한국 음식을 만들었어요. 불고기하고 떡볶이를 만들어서 친구하고 같이 먹었어요.

레이첼: 한국에도 추수감사절이 있어요?

윤호: 추수감사절하고 비슷한 명절이 있어요. 추석이라고 해요.

레이첼: 추석이 언제예요?

윤호: 추석은 음력 8월 15일이에요.

레이첼: 추석에는 보통 무슨 음식을 먹어요?

윤호: 보통 송편을 먹어요.

레이첼: **송-편**? 송편이 뭐예요?

윤호: 송편은 떡이에요. **반-달**처럼 생겼어요. 이렇게요. (반달 모양을 그린다).

레이첼: 그럼, 추석에는 보통 뭐 해요?

윤호: 가족들과 함께 윷놀이를 해요. 우리 같이 윷놀이를 해 볼까요?

Video clip

Part 3

> ## Word check-up
>
> | | | |
> |---|---|---|
> | 만들었어요 (만들다) | (v.) | to make; to prepare for food (past tense) |
> | 비슷한 | (adj.) | similar |
> | 명절 名節 | (n.) | national holiday |
> | 추석 秋夕 | (n.) | a major Korean holiday celebrated on the 15th day of the eighth month of the lunar calendar |
> | 언제예요? | | When is it? |
> | 음력 陰曆 | (n.) | lunar calendar |
> | 8월 | (n.) | August |
> | 송편 松- | (n.) | half-moon shaped Korean rice cake |
> | 떡 | (n.) | rice cake |
> | 반달 | (n.) | a half-moon; 반 半 half |
> | ~처럼 | | like/as/so . . . as |
> | 생겼어요 (생기다) | (v.) | to look like (past tense) |
> | 이렇게 | (adv.) | like this |
> | 모양 模樣 | (n.) | shape |
> | 그리다 | (v.) | to draw an image of things/person |
> | 함께 | (adv.) | together (= 같이) |
> | 윷놀이 | (n.) | a traditional Korean game (see "Activity 2" for further information) |
> | 해 볼까요? | | Shall we try? |

Grammar and expressions

1 무슨 음식? What kind of food?

'무슨' + noun structure is used to express "what kind of ~" as shown in 무슨 음식을 좋아해요? (What kind of food do you like?) 무슨 영화를 좋아해요? (What kind of movie do you like?)

마이클: 제니퍼 씨, 무슨 운동을 좋아해요? Jennifer, what kind of sports do you like?
제니퍼: 저는 배구를 좋아해요. 마이클 씨는요? I like volleyball. And you?
마이클: 저는 축구를 아주 좋아해요. I like soccer very much.

[Practice]

Let's practice this structure (무슨 + noun) with the following questions.

1 무슨 영화를 좋아해요? What kind of movies do you like?
   [e.g., 멜로 영화 romance movie; 액션 영화 action movie; 코미디 영화 comedy movie; 공포 영화 horror movie; 만화 영화 animation movie; SF 영화 science fiction movie; 전쟁 영화 war movie]
   → 저는 만화 영화를 좋아해요.
   → _____.

2 무슨 운동을 좋아해요? What kind of sports do you like?
   [e.g., 축구 soccer; 미식축구 American football; 농구 basketball; 야구 baseball; 배구 volleyball]

122

Lesson 6: Thanksgiving Day and Chuseok 추수감사절과 추석

→ 저는 축구를 좋아해요.

→ _____ .

3 무슨 음식을 좋아해요? What kind of food do you like?
[e.g., 한식 (= 한국 음식) Korean food; 중국 음식 Chinese food; 일본 음식 Japanese food; 미국 음식 American food; 이태리 음식 Italian food; 멕시코 음식 Mexican food]

→ 저는 한국 음식을 좋아해요.

→ _____ .

2 한국어로 ___ (이/가) 뭐예요? How do you say ___ in Korean? / ~(이)라고 해요. In Korean, we say ~.

How do you say "Thank you very much" in Korean? And how do you say "I am sorry" in Korean? And what about if you want to say "I study mechanical engineering" in Korean, but you don't know that particular word or phrase. In situations like these you'd like to know how to say something in Korean. As a good student of Korean, you also want to ask a question in Korean. Here is the question for you in Korean: 한국어로 _____ (이/가) 뭐예요?

Here is a dialogue between Michael and Yuna:

마이클: 유나 씨, 한국어로 <u>Christmas</u> 가 뭐예요? How do you say *Christmas* in Korean?
유나: 네, <u>크-리-스-마-스 라고 해요</u>. In Korean, we say 크-리-스-마-스 (CH-RI-S-MA-S).
마이클: 네?

Here is another dialogue between Damee and Thomas using these structures:

토마스: 다미 씨, 한국어로 *parents*가 뭐예요?
다미: 부모님이라고 해요.
토마스: 그럼, 한국어로 *professor*가 뭐예요?
다미: 교수라고 해요.
토마스: 그럼, 한국어로 *stethoscope*가 뭐예요?
다미: 네? 어, 아! *청진기* 라고 해요.

For inquiry, you ask in Korean 한국어로 _____ 뭐예요? (Here 한국어로 means "using Korean" or "in Korean"; 한국어 the Korean language is combined with a particle ~로 whose meaning is "using," "via," or "in"). The response is "_____(이)라고 해요," which is translated as "In Korean we say _____." With this structure, you notice that there are variants: ~이라고 해요 and ~라고 해요.

~이라고 해요 vs. ~라고 해요?
When the word in question ends with a <u>consonant</u> (e.g., 부모<u>님</u>), the Korean word is followed by ~이라고 해요. However, when the word ends with a <u>vowel</u> (such as 교<u>수</u>), then, the word is followed by ~라고 해요 as shown in the earlier example.

[Practice 1]

Before we move on to the next structure, let's make sure that we understand and thus use these structures properly. Using the pictures provided, ask your Korean friends how to say these animals in Korean: "한국어로 뭐예요?"

123

Part 3

Image created by authors with pixabay.com

[Practice 2]

Using the following table of college majors, ask your classmates about their majors. Your classmates will answer the question in return.

Question: 한국어로 _____ (이/가) 뭐예요?
Answer: _____ (이)라고 해요.

History 역사학	English 영어학	Math 수학	Psychology 심리학
Nursing 간호학	Business administration 경영학	Accounting 회계학	Linguistics 언어학
Education 교육학	Biology 생물학	Chemistry 화학	Physics 물리학
East Asian Studies 동아시아학	International Studies 국제학	Engineering 공학	Sociology 사회학

3 불고기하고 떡볶이 "A and B"

The word '하고' connects two words and is similar to "and" in English. For example, you make a list – let's say, for grocery shopping – using ~하고:

과일: 사과**하고** 배 (fruit: apple *and* pear)
채소: 당근**하고** 시금치 (vegetable: carrot *and* spinach)
음료수: 물**하고** 우유**하고** 오렌지 주스 (drinks: water *and* milk *and* orange juice)

   There is another way of connecting two (or more) words in Korean: using **~와/과**. We repeat the grocery shopping list using this alternative.

과일: 사과**와** 배 (fruit: apple AND pear)
채소: 당근**과** 시금치 (vegetable: carrot AND spinach)
음료수: 물**과** 우유**와** 오렌지 주스 (drinks: water AND milk AND orange juice)

Lesson 6: Thanksgiving Day and Chuseok 추수감사절과 추석

The usage of ~와/과 is the same as ~하고, and the alternation between 와 and 과 totally depends on the ending form of the preceding words: That is, the vowel-ending words (e.g., 사과, 우유) are followed by '와' whereas the consonant-ending word (e.g., 당근, 물) is followed by '과'.

Don't confuse these with the use of the sentence connective: 그리고.

1 불고기가 맛있어요. **그리고** 떡볶이도 맛있어요. (linking two sentences with 그리고)
2 불고기**하고** 떡볶이가 맛있어요. (linking two words with ~하고)

Cultural notes

When is Chuseok?

New Year's Day and Chuseok are two major national holidays that everybody celebrates in Korea. Chuseok (추석) is most Koreans' favorite holiday. When is Chuseok? And what is it? It is similar to Thanksgiving in the United States. Specifically, Chuseok is celebrated on the 15th of the eighth month of the lunar calendar (음력). People in South Korea celebrate 추석 for three days (Chuseok Day and the previous and following days). They often visit their hometowns to celebrate the holiday with family members. As part of the celebration, many people prepare many foods ahead of time that are usually made of that year's new crops. Then, on Chuseok Day, they have a ceremonial dinner to commemorate their ancestors. They also pay a visit to their ancestors' tombs during the holiday. As mentioned in the Lesson 6 dialogues, Koreans enjoy a special kind of rice cake called '송편'. Although 송편 can be made in many shapes, a typical shape resembles a half moon. Traditionally, the rice cake is steamed with pine needles (the part of the word 송 means "pine tree").

4 추석(이) 언제예요? When is Chuseok?

Now that we know a little bit about 추석, we need to say when the holiday is in Korean. Again, when is Chuseok? Chuseok is celebrated on the 15th of the eighth month of the lunar calendar.

Question: 추석이 언제예요?
Answer: 음력으로 8월 15일이에요.

(음력 lunar calendar; 음력으로 by the lunar calendar)

Let's first talk about **months of the year** in Korean:

일 월 January	이 월 February	삼 월 March	사 월 April	오 월 May	유 월 June
칠 월 July	팔 월 August	구 월 September	시 월 October	십일 월 November	십이 월 December

The months of the year in Korean are named according to their number (from one to 12) using Sino-Korean numbers: 일 월 (1 + 월 "month") to 십이 월 (12 + 월 "month"). Depending on the

125

Part 3

months, we have either 30 or 31 days in a month (except for 2월, February), and we count the days using Sino-Korean numbers 일 일, 이 일, 삼 일 . . .삽십 일, 삼십일 일 (i.e., Sino-Korean numbers + 일 "day"). As marked in blue, for the sake of pronunciation, June and October should be read as 유 월 (*not* 육 월) and 시월 (*not* 십 월).

[Practice]

As shown in the example, read the following months and days in Korean.
Sample sentence: 1월 17일 → 일 월 십칠 일이에요.

1 11월 26일 → _____ .
2 6월 9일 → _____ .
3 10월 13일 → _____ .
4 생일이 언제예요? (When is your birthday? Write it in Korean.)
   → _____ .

Let's talk about days of the week in Korean:

일요일	Sunday
월요일	Monday
화요일	Tuesday
수요일	Wednesday
목요일	Thursday
금요일	Friday
토요일	Saturday

As shown each day (일-월-화-수-목-금-토 Sunday through Saturday) is followed by the word 요일 (meaning "day' or "date").
Here is a conversation between Michael and Damee regarding days of the week:

다미: 오늘은 무슨 요일이에요? What is the day of the week today?
마이클: 네? What?
다미: 오늘은 화요일이에요? 수요일이에요? Is today Tuesday or Wednesday?
마이클: 아, 오늘은 목요일이에요. Ah, it is Thursday today.
다미: 그럼, 내일은 무슨 요일이에요? Then, what is the day of the week tomorrow?
마이클: 네, 내일은 금요일이에요. Tomorrow is Friday.
다미: 모레는 무슨 요일이에요? What is the day of the week the day after tomorrow?
마이클: 모레는 토요일이에요. It is Saturday.
다미: 마이클 씨, 토요일에 바빠요? Michael, are you busy on Saturday?
마이클: 네, 바빠요. Yes, I am.
다미: 그럼, 일요일은요? Then, how about Sunday?
마이클: 일요일은 괜찮아요. 왜요? Sunday will be fine. Why?
다미: 우리 같이 영화봐요. Let's go to a movie together.
마이클: 네, 좋아요. 무슨 영화를 좋아해요? Sounds good. What kind of movie would you like?

126

Lesson 6: Thanksgiving Day and Chuseok 추수감사절과 추석

2017년 10월

일	월	화	수	목	금	토
1	2	3 개천절	4 추석	5 추석연휴	6	7
8	9 한글날	10	11	12	13	14
15	16	17	18	19	20	21
22	23	24	25	26	27	28
29	30	31				

> ### A Korean calendar
> Image created by authors

[Practice]

Look at the calendar and answer the following questions.

1 오늘은 시 월 십이 일이에요. 오늘은 무슨 요일이에요? _____ .
2 오늘은 시 월 이십사 일이에요. 오늘은 무슨 요일이에요? _____ .
3 오늘은 시 월 칠 일이에요. 오늘은 무슨 요일이에요? _____ .
4 오늘은 추석이에요. 오늘은 무슨 요일이에요? _____ .

5 추석에 뭐 했어요? What did you do on Chuseok?

In Lesson 5, we studied the ways in which we make a verb past-tense in Korean. As we say, "Practice makes perfect." Let's review what we have learned from Lesson 5: How do we make a verb past-tense in Korean?

Let's use the basic/dictionary form '먹다' to eat, '가다' to go.

Step 1: From the basic forms, conjugate the verbs into present-tense forms.
  먹다 → 먹어요
  가다 → 가요
Step 2: From the conjugated forms in present tense, drop ~요 → 먹어 – ; 가.
Step 3: To those forms, add ㅆ어요 → 먹어 + ㅆ어요; 가 + ㅆ어요.
Step 4: You now have the conjugated forms in past tense → 먹었어요; 갔어요.

By now, you are ready to answer the question "What did you do last night?" as shown:

마이클: 어젯밤에 뭐 했어요? What did you do last night? (어젯밤 last night)
제니퍼: 어젯밤에 한국어 공부를 했어요. I studied Korean last night.
탐: 어젯밤에 비디오 게임을 했어요. I played video games last night.
미나: 어젯밤에 친구한테 이메일을 했어요. I emailed my friends last night. (친구한테 to friends)

[Practice]

Ask your classmates the following questions.

1 어젯밤 10시에 뭐 했어요? _____ .
2 어제 오전 9시에 뭐 했어요? _____ .

127

Part 3

3 어제 오후 5시에 어디에 갔어요? _____ .
4 어제 저녁에 뭐 먹었어요? _____ .
5 어제 저녁에 누구하고 먹었어요? _____ .

6   반달처럼 생겼어요. It is shaped like a crescent-moon.

As mentioned in the previous section, 송편 is a delicious Korean rice cake, 떡, which Koreans enjoy on Chuseok. It looks like a crescent-moon, or is shaped like a half-moon. In this section, we will learn about the structure '[noun] + 처럼' such that you can make a comparison between two items or two people that look like each other. ~처럼 literally means "like" or "as if"; thus '[noun] + 처럼' means that something or someone looks like or is shaped like the [noun]. Here are some example sentences with this structure.

1 마이클 씨는 **탐 크루즈처럼** 생겼어요. Michal looks like Tom Cruise.
2 다미 씨는 **고양이처럼** 생겼어요. Damee looks like a cat.

You look like Elvis
Pixabay.com

Elvis Presley was probably one of the most famous American celebrities, so well known that he has "look-alike" impersonators worldwide. To the question "누구처럼 생겼어요?", the impersonators definitely want to hear "엘비스 프레슬리처럼 생겼어요" (You look like Elvis Presley).

Lesson 6: Thanksgiving Day and Chuseok 추수감사절과 추석

[Practice]

Look at the pictures and answer the following question.

Question: 뭐 (= 무엇)처럼 생겼어요?
Answer: _____ 처럼 생겼어요.

It looks like _____
Pixabay.com

It looks like _____
Pixabay.com

7   떡볶이를 만들*어서* 친구하고 같이 먹었어요: ~어서/아서
two events sequentially connected

In this section, we will show you how two events are sequentially connected with ~어서/아서. Let's begin with some examples:

1   학교에 <u>가서</u> 공부를 해요. (Event A, 학교에 가요 → then Event B, 공부를 해요)
2   집에 <u>가서</u> 숙제를 했어요. (Event A, 집에 갔어요 → then Event B, 숙제를 했어요)
3   친구를 <u>만나서</u> 영화를 봤어요. (Event A, 친구를 만났어요 → then Event B, [친구하고] 영화를 봤어요)

　　Two events are related and also sequentially connected. By "sequentially connected," we mean that Event A precedes Event B (not the other way around). Each event is connected with ~어서/아서, and these events are temporally or sequentially related.

129

Part 3

The same structure can be used to describe two events with cause and effect, meaning that one event causes another event or one event provides a reason for the following event. This use of ~어서/아서 will be further explained in later chapters.

1 늦어서 미안합니다. I am sorry for being late.
2 마이클 씨는 키가 커서 농구를 잘 해요. Because Michael is tall, he plays basketball well.

8   윷놀이 게임을 해 볼까요? Shall we play a game?

The structure ~(으)ㄹ까요? invites the listener's opinion on or participation in the event the speaker is talking about. It may also be used as a question, but it functions as a mild (or indirect) suggestion or invitation. With this structure, both speaker and listener agree and thus do things together, as shown in the dialogue between Michael and Amy.

마이클: 저녁에 뭐 먹을까요? What would you like to have for dinner tonight?
에이미: 글쎄요. 피자를 먹을까요? Let's see . . . shall we have some pizza? (글쎄요 well, let's see)
마이클: 네, 좋아요. Sounds good.

Here is another conversation between Yoon-ho and Rachel.

윤호: 주말에 영화를 볼까요, 쇼핑을 할까요? Shall we go to a movie or go shopping over the weekend? (주말 weekend)
레이첼: 영화봐요. Let's go to a movie.
윤호: 좋아요. 무슨 영화를 볼까요? Good. What kind of movie would you like to go to?
레이첼: 액션 영화를 봐요. Let's watch an action movie.

Depending on the stem form, you may have to add the vowel 으 to the structure: 먹 – 으 + ㄹ까요? → 먹을까요? vs. 보 + ㄹ까요? → 볼까요?
You can also use this structure ~(으)ㄹ까요? for asking or inquiring about the listener's own opinion or thoughts exclusively (to be discussed in later chapters):

마이클: 다미 씨, 내일 비가 올까요? Damee, (do you think) it will rain tomorrow?
다미: 글쎄요. Let's see (or Well . . .).
마이클: 다미 씨, 창문을 닫을까요? Shall I close the window?
다미: 네, 그러세요. Please do so.

Yut, a traditional Korean game
Getty Image Bank royalty-free image

Lesson 6: Thanksgiving Day and Chuseok 추수감사절과 추석

Exercises

● As shown in the example, complete the following dialogues.

[Example]

윤호: 오늘 저녁에 <u>무슨 음식을 시킬까요</u>?
린다: 불고기 어때요?
윤호: 좋아요. 떡볶이도 시켜요.

1 마이클: 무슨 영화를 좋아해요?
   민지: _____ .
2 탐: 보통 무슨 책을 읽어요?
   미나:_____ .
3 민지: 보통 무슨 운동을 해요?
   You: _____ .

● Choose the correct answer from the choices given.

[Choices]

가. 네, 인형처럼 생겼어요. (인형 doll)
나. 네, 반달처럼 생겼어요.
다. 네, 농구 선수처럼 키가 커요.

4 마이클 씨 여자 친구 만났어요?
   → _____ .
5 제니퍼 씨 남자 친구를 알아요?
   → _____ .
6 송편이 뭐예요?
   → _____ .

● Answer the following questions in Korean.

7 어제 저녁에 뭐 먹었어요?
   → _____ .
8 어젯밤 9시에 뭐 했어요?
   → _____ .
9 지난 주말에 어디에 갔어요?
   → _____ .
10 지난 금요일에 뭐 공부했어요?
   → _____ .

● Answer the questions with the correct answer from the given choices, as shown in the example.

[Choices] 문화, 역사, 문학, 명절, 취미

한국어로 history (이/가) 뭐예요? → 역사라고 해요.

11 한국어로 culture (이/가) 뭐예요?
   → _____ .
12 한국어로 hobbies (이/가) 뭐예요?
   → _____ .
13 한국어로 national holidays (이/가) 뭐예요?
   → _____ .

131

Part 3

Cultural notes

On your way home for Chuseok

To celebrate Chuseok with their relatives, many Koreans travel to their hometown. People usually wear traditional clothes called *Hanbok* (한복). Most of the time young couples with their children visit their parents who are living in rural areas. Therefore, during the Chuseok holiday, it is quite challenging to buy tickets for public transportation (e.g., bus, train, or airplane). However, it is always a joy to visit and have a good time with family and friends on Chuseok.

Activity 1

Role play: Thanksgiving Day

여러분과 친구가 레이첼과 윤호의 역할극을 해요. 레이첼이 윤호에게 추수감사절을 소개해요. 윤호가 레이첼에게 추석을 소개해요.
You and your partner will role play the parts of Rachel and Yoon-ho. Rachel introduces Thanksgiving Day to Yoon-ho. Yoon-ho introduces Chuseok to Rachel.

Thanksgiving 추수 감사절

turkey	칠면조
apple pie	사과파이
potato	감자
pumpkin	호박

Chuseok 추석

rice cake	송편
dried persimmon	곶감
dumpling	만두
pear	배

Images related to Thanksgiving
Pixabay.com

Lesson 6: Thanksgiving Day and Chuseok 추수감사절과 추석

Images related to Thanksgiving
Pixabay.com

윤호: 추수감사절에는 보통 무슨 음식을 먹어요? What do people usually eat on Thanksgiving?
레이첼: 추수감사절에는 <u>turkey</u> (을/를) 먹어요. People eat turkey.
윤호: <u>Turkey</u> (이/가) 한국어로 뭐예요? How do you say *turkey* in Korean?
레이첼: <u>칠면조</u>예요. It is said **칠**-**면**-**조**.
레이첼: 추석에는 보통 무슨 음식을 먹어요? What do people usually eat on Chuseok?
윤호: 추석에는 <u>rice cake</u> (을/를) 먹어요. People eat rice cakes.
레이첼: <u>Rice cake</u> (이/가) 한국어로 뭐예요? How do you say *rice cake* in Korean?
윤호: <u>송편</u>이에요. It is said 송-편.

133

Part 3

> **Activity 2**
>
> ### Let's play Yut
>
> 윷놀이는 한국의 전통 놀이예요. 두 명이 한 팀이에요. 두 팀 씩 윷놀이를 해 볼까요? Yut is a traditional Korean folk game. Yut game is usually played between two partners or two teams. But, you can invite more teams to play together.
>
>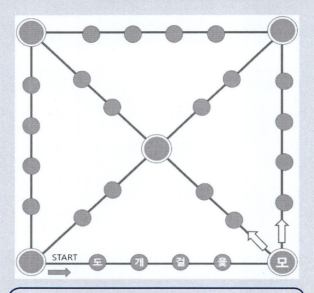
>
> The board (mal-pan, 말판) of the Yut game
> Image created by authors
>
> The Korean game Yut is a traditional board game played in Korea. Although the origins of this popular family game are unclear, some research suggests that Yut was played as early as the Three Kingdoms (57 BCE – 668 CE). There is a folk explanation for the game that describes a bet by some villagers during that period who raised five different kinds of livestock: pigs, dogs, sheep, cows, and horses.[1]

Vocabulary expansion

밑줄 친 단어를 보세요. 박스 안에 있는 단어를 사용해서 다음의 대화를 연습하세요. Please look at the underlined words. Use the words in the box to practice the following conversations.

Holidays

윤호: 안녕하세요?
레이첼: 안녕하세요. 만나서 반가워요.
윤호: **미국 독립기념일** 에는 보통 무엇을 해요?
레이첼: **미국 독립기념일**에는 보통 **불꽃놀이** (fireworks) **를 해요**.
윤호: 그래요? **한국독립기념일** 에는 보통 **국기** (flag) **를 달아요**.

Lesson 6: Thanksgiving Day and Chuseok 추수감사절과 추석

독립기념일 Independence Day

성조기 US flag
Pixabay.com

7월 4일 Fourth of July
성조기 US flag
불꽃놀이 fireworks
쇼핑 shopping

한글날 Hangeul Proclamation Day

세종대왕 King Sejong
Pixabay.com

135

Part 3

10월 9일
세종대왕 King Sejong
붓글씨 calligraphy
한국어 공부 studying Korean

성탄절 Christmas

성탄절 트리 Christmas tree
Pixabay.com

12월 25일
트리 tree
양말 socks
선물 gifts

Translations of Dialogues I and II

Dialogue 1

Yoon-ho: Rachel! What did you do on Thanksgiving?
Rachel: I went to my home in Chicago.
Yoon-ho: What do you usually eat on *Chusugamsajeol*?
Rachel: What? Chu-su-gam-sa-jeol? What is Chusugamsajeol?
Yoon-ho: Ah, Thanksgiving Day is *Chu-su-gam-sa-jeol* in Korean.
Rachel: Ah, I see. Then, what is turkey in Korean?
Yoon-ho: Turkey is *Chil-myun-jo* in Korean.
Rachel: *Chil-myun-jo*. Yes. People usually eat turkey and pie. I ate lots of turkey and pumpkin pie this past Thanksgiving Day. They were very delicious.
Yoon-ho: Then? What did you?
Rachel: There is a huge sale on Thanksgiving Day. So after dinner with my family, we went shopping at a department store. I bought a big television as well.

Dialogue 2

Rachel: By the way, what did you do on Thanksgiving Day?

Yoon-ho: I cooked Korean food with my friends. I made *bulgogi* and *tteokbokki* and ate them with my friends.

Rachel: Do you have Thanksgiving Day in Korea?

Yoon-ho: We have a holiday similar to Thanksgiving Day. It is called *Chuseok*.

Rachel: When is the *Chuseok*?

Yoon-ho: *Chuseok* is the 15th of August on the lunar calendar.

Rachel: What kind of food do people usually eat on Chuseok?

Yoon-ho: People usually eat *songpyeon*.

Rachel: Song-pyeon? What is songpeyon?

Yoon-ho: Songpyeon is a rice cake. It is shaped like a crescent moon, like this (he draws the crescent-moon).

Rachel: Then, what do people usually do on Chuseok?

Yoon-ho: People play the traditional Korean game, Yut. Let's play the game together.

Note

1 https://en.wikipedia.org/wiki/Yut

Lesson 7

Korean markets and college clubs/student organizations
한인 마트와 대학 동아리

Learning goals

- Explain a purpose for going places.
- Use future-tense forms.
- Describe actions in progress.

Grammar and expressions

- 김치를 먹어 보세요. Try something new.
- 같이 갈 수 있어요? Are you available to go with me?
- 어떡하지요? What shall I do? (There is nothing I can do about it.)
- 사진을 찍으러 호수에 갔어요. In order to take pictures, we went to the lake.
- 안경을 썼어요. I wore glasses. (to wear 쓰다; 입다; 신다)
- 태권도를 배우고 있어요. I am learning Taekwondo. (= Things are in progress.)
- 처음에 힘들었는데 . . . It was difficult at first but . . .
- 물어볼게요. I will ask her/him (about this).

139

Part 3

Activities

- Visiting local Korean markets
- My social networks

Cultural notes

- Korean street foods
- Korean markets in the United States
- Student clubs and organizations

Vocabulary expansion

- Words for college clubs

Lesson 7: Korean markets and college clubs 한인 마트와 대학 동아리

DIALOGUE 1

Wow, it's delicious. 와, 맛있어요

Yoon-ho introduces Rachel to a Korean grocery market.

레이첼: 윤호 씨, 지금 뭐 먹어요?

윤호: 초코파이를 먹어요. 한인 마트에서 샀어요. 한번 먹어 보세요. 여기요.

레이첼: 와, 맛있어요. 그런데 한인 마트가 어디에 있어요?

윤호: 파크 스트리트 (Park St.) 에 있어요. 그리고 유니버시티 에비뉴 (University Ave.) 에도 하나 있어요.

레이첼: 그래요? 몰랐어요. 저도 초코파이를 사고 싶어요. 윤호 씨, 오늘 저랑 같이 한인 마트에 갈 수 있어요?

윤호: 어떡하지요? 오늘은 친구하고 약속이 있어요. 동아리 친구하고 같이 사진을 찍으러 멘도타 (Mendota) 호수에 갈 거예요. 다음에 같이 가요.

레이첼: 그래요? 그럼, 다음에 꼭 같이 가요. 다음에 꼭!

윤호: 네, 정말 미안해요. 다음에 꼭 같이 가요.

Video clip

Part 3

Word check-up

초코파이	(n.)	Choco-pie (moon pie)
파크 스트리트	(n.)	Park Street
유니버시티 에버뉴	(n.)	University Avenue
한인 마트 韓人 market	(n.)	Korean grocery store
샀어요 (사다)	(v.)	to buy (past tense)
와	(excl.)	wow
몰랐어요 (모르다)	(v.)	don't know (past tense)
어디(에)	(at)	where
저랑 같이		together with me
~수 있다	(v.)	can do/be able to ~
어떡하지요?		What should I do?
오늘	(n, adv.)	today
약속 約束	(n.)	promise/appointment
동아리	(n.)	college clubs/organizations
호수 湖水	(n.)	lake
다음에	(adv.)	next time
꼭	(adv.)	surely/certainly/for sure
미안해요		I am sorry

Lesson 7: Korean markets and college clubs 한인 마트와 대학 동아리

DIALOGUE 2

I am learning Taekwondo 태권도를 배우고 있어요

Yoon-ho shows Rachel a picture he took the last weekend with his friend from a student organization, and they talk about the activities of different student organizations on campus.

윤호: 레이첼 씨, 이 사진을 좀 보세요.

레이첼: 무슨 사진이에요?

윤호: 지난 주말에 찍은 사진이에요 멘도타 호수에서 친구하고 같이 찍었어요. 여기 안경 쓴 사람이 제 여자 친구예요.

레이첼: 윤호 씨, 여자 친구가 있어요? 몰랐어요. 음, 여자 친구(가) 아주 예뻐요. 그런데 여자 친구 이름이 뭐예요?

윤호: 유나예요. 유나하고 사진 동아리에서 처음 만났어요. 레이첼 씨도 동아리가 있어요?

레이첼: 그럼요. 태권도 동아리에서 태권도를 배우고 있어요. 태권도가 처음에는 많이 힘들었는데 지금은 아주 재미있어요. 그런데, 사실 한국 춤도 배우고 싶어요.

윤호: 춤 동아리도 있어요. 참, 유나가 춤 동아리 회장이에요. 제가 유나한테 한번 물어볼게요.

레이첼: 아, 그래요. 감사합니다.

Video clip

143

Part 3

Word check-up

무슨		what kind of/which
사진 寫眞	(n.)	a photo
찍었어요 (찍다)	(v.)	take (a photo) (past tense)
지난 주말 週末	(n.)	last weekend
안경 眼鏡	(n.)	eye glasses
썼어요 (쓰다)	(v.)	to wear
사람	(n.)	a person, someone
여자 친구 女子 親舊	(n.)	girlfriend
예뻐요 (예쁘다)	(adj.)	to be pretty
동아리	(n.)	a student organization
처음	(n., adv.)	the first (time)
만났어요 (만나다)	(v.)	to meet (past tense)
태권도 跆拳道	(n.)	Taekwondo
배우고 있어요 (배우다)	(v.)	be learning
힘들었는데 (힘들다)	(adj.)	to be difficult/to have a hard time
지금 只今	(n.)	now
춤	(n.)	dance
회장 會長	(n.)	president, head (of a group)
미나한테 (person + 한테)		to Mina
물어볼게요 (물어보다)	(v.)	to try to ask

Grammar and expressions

1   김치를 먹어 보세요. Try kimchee

The structure verb stem + '어/아 보세요' is used to suggest (or propose) that the listener should try something new or things he/she has not yet tried. Here are specific examples:

1   Tom has never tried Korean food, so his friend Mira encourages him to try to have some Korean food such as bulgogi 불고기 or bibimbop 비빔밥.

탐:　　저는 한국 음식을 잘 몰라요.
미라:　그래요? 그럼, 불고기를 먹어 보세요. 먹~ (to eat) + 어 보세요 (try to . . .)
탐:　　불고기요?
미라:　네, 아주 맛있어요.

2   Mike loves coffee. He also wants to try some authentic Korean tea, so he asks Minjee about Korean tea.

마이클:　저는 보통 커피를 마셔요. 그런데 한국 차는 어때요?
민지:　　한국 차도 맛있어요. 혹시 인삼차 알아요? (혹시 by any chance)
마이클:　인삼차요? 아니요, 몰라요.
민지:　　그럼, 인삼차를 한번 마셔 보세요. 마시~ (to drink) + 어 보세요 (try to . . .)

　　　　　Verb stem + ~어 보세요 (or ~아 보세요) try to

144

Lesson 7: Korean markets and college clubs 한인 마트와 대학 동아리

먹-다: 먹 + 어 보세요 → 불고기를 먹어 보세요 Please try to eat . . .
마시-다: 마시 + 어 보세요 → 인삼차를 마셔 보세요 Please try to drink . . .

The part ~어/아 보세요 politely encourages listeners to try to take actions which are indicated by the verbs (here, 먹-다 and 마시-다). The combination of "action" in the verbs and encouragement expressed in ~어/아 보세요 means "Try this or that which you've never done before" in a polite way. Let's practice this combination step-by-step using the verbs 하다, 배우다, 가다, 듣다.

Basic form	Step 1: Conjugate form in present tense	Step 2: Drop ~요	Step 3: Attach ~ 보세요
하다 to do	해요	해~	해 보세요
배우다 to learn	배워요	배워~	배워 보세요
가다 to go	가요	가 ~	가 보세요
듣다 to listen to	들어요	들어~	들어 보세요

Here are sample sentences with the combinations you have just worked on.

1 번지점프를 해 보세요. (번지점프 bungee jumping)
2 한국어를 배워 보세요.
3 제주도에 가 보세요.
4 케이팝 (K-pop)을 들어 보세요.

[Practice]

Using the structure ~어/아 보세요, ask your classmates to do something they have never tried before.

2 같이 갈 수 있어요? Are you available to go with me?

Sometimes you might wonder whether your friend is available to do things with you (such as playing tennis, watching a movie, having a meal, etc.). The structure ~(으)ㄹ 수 있어요 is used for that.

1 In a question, '~(으)ㄹ 수 있어요?' asks about the availability of your friend:
   테니스를 같이 칠 수 있어요? (치~ + ㄹ 수 있어요?)
   영화를 같이 볼 수 있어요? (보~ + ㄹ 수 있어요?)
   같이 식사할 수 있어요? (식사하~ + ㄹ 수 있어요?)

   In response, the other party answers you with their availability:

   네, 테니스를 칠 수 있어요. I am available to play tennis (with you).
   네, 영화를 볼 수 있어요.
   네, 같이 식사할 수 있어요.

2 '~(으)ㄹ 수 있어요?' can also be used to express capability or ability:

   한국어 책을 읽을 수 있어요? (읽~ + (으) ㄹ 수 있어요?)
   한국 음식을 요리할 수 있어요? (요리하~ + ㄹ 수 있어요?)
   매운 음식을 먹을 수 있어요? (먹~ (으) ㄹ 수 있어요?; 매운 hot/spicy; 매운 음식 spicy food)

145

Part 3

Depending on your capability or ability, you may or may not be able to do things:

네, 한국어 책을 읽을 수 **있어요**. OR 아니요, 한국어 책을 읽을 수 **없어요.**
네, 한국 음식을 요리할 수 있어요. OR 아니요, 한국 음식을 요리할 수 없어요.
네, 매운 음식을 먹을 수 있어요. OR 아니요, 매운 음식을 먹을 수 없어요.

As for this structure, when the stem ends with a consonant (e.g., 먹 – ; 읽 –), the vowel '으' is inserted and ~ㄹ 수 있어요 is attached to the verb stem. Compare this structure when used with a vowel-ending stem and a consonant-ending stem.

Vowel-ending stem + ~ㄹ 수 있어요	*Consonant-ending stem + 으 + ~ㄹ 수 있어요*
가다: 갈 수 있어요	먹다: 먹을 수 있어요
하다: 할 수 있어요	읽다: 읽을 수 있어요

Here is a dialogue between Michael and Minjee.

마이클:　민지 씨, 주말에 시간 있어요? (주말 weekend)
민지:　　네, 토요일에 시간 있어요. 왜요? (토요일 Saturday)
마이클:　불고기가 먹고 싶어요. 불고기를 요리할 수 있어요?
민지:　　그럼요. 불고기를 요리할 수 있어요.
마이클:　잡채도 요리할 수 있어요?
민지:　　잡채는 요리할 수 없어요. 미안해요.

[Practice 1]

Ask your classmates if they can cook Korean food: 한국 음식을 요리할 수 있어요?

저랑 같이 갈 수 있어요? (= 저하고 같이 갈 수 있어요?)

'~(이)랑' (as in '저랑') is a colloquial form of '하고' meaning "together with (someone or something)," as shown:

1　저랑 같이 테니스 칠 수 있어요? (= 저하고 같이 테니스를 칠 수 있어요?)
2　저랑 같이 커피를 마실 수 있어요? (= 저하고 같이 커피를 마실 수 있어요?)

Also, '~(이)랑' lists or links more than two nouns:

3　한인 마트에서 사과랑 배랑 과자를 샀어요. (사과 apple; 배 pear; 과자 snack)
4　마이클이랑 제니랑 미나는 친한 친구예요. (친한 친구 close friends, best friends)

As shown, the variation between '~랑' and '~이랑' depends on the ending of the preceding nouns: That is, 마이클 (consonant-ending '클') is paired with ~이랑 while 제니 (vowel-ending '니') is accompanied by ~랑.

[Practice 2]

Answer the following questions using ~랑/이랑.

1　누구랑 같이 영화를 보고 싶어요? → _____ .
2　누구랑 같이 여행을 하고 싶어요? → _____ .
3　누구랑 같이 저녁 식사를 하고 싶어요? → _____ .

Lesson 7: Korean markets and college clubs 한인 마트와 대학 동아리

3 어떡하지요? What shall I do? (= There is nothing I can do about it.)

The expression "어떡하지요?" is often used when you encounter a problem or situation in which you almost feel like there is nothing you can do about it to turn things around. This expression originates from '어떻게 하다' which means "to do things in certain way": 어떻게 하다 → 어떠하다 → 어떡하지요? By putting this in a question "어떡하지요?" you express that you are facing a situation which you have no control over and thus, you feel frustrated: "What shall I do under the circumstance?" At this point, you might also wonder what this ~지요 ending means. Here are some example sentences.

1 제니 씨가 예뻐요? Is Jenny pretty?
2 제니 씨가 예쁘지요? Jenny is pretty, isn't she?

As shown, the question "제니 씨가 예뻐요?" is asking for factual information regarding the situation whereas the question "제니 씨가 예쁘지요?" is seeking for the listener's agreement with what the speaker has just said. With the '~지요?', the speaker actually expects the listener's confirmation on the situation which the speaker expresses or comments on. Putting this into the current expression "어떡하지요?", the speaker invites the listener's compassion regarding the situation.

Here are sample dialogues between Michael and Damee with this expression.

마이클: 어떡하지요? 수업에 늦었어요. What shall I do? I am late for class.
다미: 수업이 몇 시에 있어요? When is the class?
마이클: 오전 9 시예요. 그런데 지금은 벌써 9 시 10 분이에요. It is at 9am. But it is already 9:10 am.
다미: 어서 가세요. Hurry and go.
마이클: 내일 시간 있어요? 다미 씨하고 같이 영화를 보고 싶어요.
다미: 어떡하지요? 내일 아르바이트가 있어요. 그래서 아주 바빠요.
마이클: 그래요? 그럼, 다음에 같이 영화를 봐요.

4 사진을 찍으러 호수에 갔어요 In order to take pictures, we went to a lake

In this section, we will talk about the structure ~러 or ~으러. This structure ~(으)러 is usually accompanied by the verb '가다' indicating that you go some places with certain purposes in mind, and ~(으)러 specifies the purposes as shown here.

1 친구를 만나러 커피숍에 갔어요. I went to a coffee shop in order to meet my friends.
2 책을 빌리러 도서관에 갔어요. I went to the library in order to borrow books.
3 수업을 들으러 밴 하이즈에 갔어요. I went to Van Hise in order to attend a class.
4 점심을 먹으러 학교식당에 갔어요. I went to the school cafeteria in order to have lunch.

→ ~(으)러 [places]에 갔어요: You went to [places] *for the purpose of* [doing things].

The variation between ~러 and ~으러 depends on the ending of each verb: for example, 만나 – (다) ends with a vowel and thus attach ~러 (만나 + ~러: 만나러) while since the stem in 먹 – (다) ends with a consonant, add the vowel (으) along with ~러 to the stem (먹 + 으러: 먹으러).

By now you have probably noticed that when verbs are conjugated, the vowel 으 is frequently inserted. This is called the 으 insertion phenomenon, and it occurs mainly to make the word easier to pronounce (i.e., ease of articulation). Given the earlier examples, we can still pronounce 만나러 and 먹러 (if we stick to the one form ~러 in this case); however, you may

147

Part 3

find it a lot easier to say '먹으러' over '먹러', and that is the driving force of the 으 – insertion you have noticed in Korean.

Here is a dialogue between Yoon-ho and Rachel.

레이첼: 윤호 씨, 지금 어디에 가요?
윤호: <u>우표를 사러</u> 우체국에 가요. 레이첼 씨는 지금 어디에 가요? (우표 stamps; 우체국 post office)
레이첼: 저는 <u>구두를 사러</u> 쇼핑몰에 가요. (구두 dress shoes)

Here is another conversation between Michael and Damee.

마이클: 다미 씨, 어제 왜 수업에 안 왔어요?
다미: <u>비자를 받으러</u> 대사관에 갔어요. 마이클 씨는 지금 어디에 가요?
마이클: <u>돈을 찾으러</u> 은행에 가요.
(비자 visa; 받다 to get issued; 대사관 embassy; 돈 money; 돈을 찾다 to take out/ withdraw money)

[Practice]

Answer the question 어디에 가요? using the clues given.

1   어디에 가요? → 도서관, 친구
2   어디에 가요? → 중국 식당, 만두 (dim sum, dumplings)
3   어디에 가요? → 백화점, 블라우스 (blouses)

5   안경을 썼어요. I am wearing glasses. (to wear – 쓰다; 입다; 신다)

This section will show that Korean has more than one word for "to wear," such as 쓰다, 입다, and 신다 depending on what you are putting on. In the dialogue in this lesson, Yoon-ho's girlfriend, Yuna, wears glasses as expressed in 유나 씨는 안경을 썼어요.

Then, how do we say that "Yuna wears a hat 모자, a blouse 블라우스, a skirt 치마, shoes 신발 and socks 양말?"

The following examples illustrate how we say them in Korean:

1   유나 씨는 모자를 썼어요. ← 쓰다
2   유나 씨는 블라우스를 입었어요. ← 입다
3   유나 씨는 치마를 입었어요. ← 입다
4   유나 씨는 신발을 신었어요. ← 신다
5   유나 씨는 양말을 신었어요. ← 신다

By now you may be overwhelmed because you have to remember which verb (for wearing or putting on) should be used depending on what you are wearing. You might wonder whether there are any rules or systematic ways in which the words (쓰다, 입다, 신다) are used.

Well, actually there are more words than 쓰다, 입다, 신다 for "to wear/put on things" in Korean. We will introduce those words in later chapters.

Wait a second! You hear these expressions for wearing things only in past tense. You might wonder if we can say 안경을 써요 in present tense, too. *Yes,* but with a different meaning and interpretation. Here is the comparison between 안경을 썼어요 and 안경을 써요:

1   유나 씨는 안경을 썼어요→ You saw Yuna woke up and put on her glasses this morning. And you know that she has been wearing glasses since this morning.
2   유나 씨는 안경을 써요→ Yuna just woke up, and you see she is putting on her glasses right NOW.

148

Lesson 7: Korean markets and college clubs 한인 마트와 대학 동아리

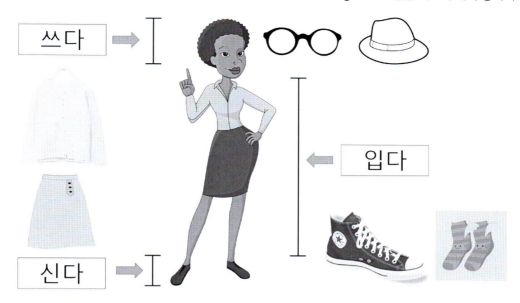

Korean words for "wearing"
Image created by authors with pixabay image

6 태권도를 배우고 있어요. I am learning Taekwondo. (= Things are in progress.)

What have you been up to these days? What are you doing right now? In English, when you are doing things at the moment or you have been involved in activities that are in progress, we use the present progressive "~ing," as in "I am studying Korean this semester" or "I have been practicing Korean every day." In this section, we are going to learn the corresponding structure in Korean. Let's begin with some example sentences.

1   지금 뭐 해요? What are you doing right now?
   → 음악을 듣고 있어요. I am *listening to* music.
   → 텔레비전을 보고 있어요. I am *watching* TV.
   → 점심을 먹고 있어요. I am *having* lunch.
   → 책을 읽고 있어요. I am *reading* a book.
   → 친구하고 전화하고 있어요. I am *talking* on the phone with my friend.

2   이번 학기에 뭐 공부해요? What have you been studying this semester?
   → 한국어를 공부하고 있어요. I have been studying Korean.
   → 한국 역사를 공부하고 있어요. I have been studying Korean history. (한국 역사 Korean history)
   → 미국 문화를 공부하고 있어요. I have been studying American culture. (미국 문화 American culture)
   → 심리학을 공부하고 있어요. I have been studying psychology. (심리학 Psychology)

As we use "verb stem + -ing" in English, so we use "verb stem + -고 있다" in Korean for expressing things which you are currently doing or things you started at some point in

149

Part 3

Food and drink
Image created by authors with pixabay image

the past and have been doing it up until the moment you talk about it (which is the present moment *now*).

[Practice]

Answer the following questions using the structure -고 있어요.

1   지금 뭐 **먹고 있어요**? → _____ .
2   지금 뭐 <u>마시고 있어요</u>? → _____ .

7   처음에는 힘들었는데 . . . It was difficult at first but . . .

Two contrasting or dissimilar concepts are compared using the sentence connective ~는데 as shown here.

1   처음에는 힘들었어요. 그런데, 지금은 괜찮아요.
    (= 처음에는 <u>힘들었는데</u> 지금은 괜찮아요)

2   키가 작았어요. 그런데 지금은 키가 아주 커요.
    (= 키가 <u>작았는데</u> 지금은 키가 아주 커요)

Lesson 7: Korean markets and college clubs 한인 마트와 대학 동아리

3 어제는 더웠어요. 그런데 지금은 좀 추워요.
  (= 어제는 <u>더웠는데</u> 지금은 좀 추워요)

4 영미는 노래를 잘 해요. 그런데 마이클은 노래를 못 해요. (노래 song)
  (= 영미는 노래를 <u>잘 하는데</u> 마이클은 노래를 못 해요)

Here is a sample dialogue between Yuna and Michael.

유나: 마이클 씨는 태권도를 아주 잘 해요.
마이클: 처음에는 <u>잘 못했는데</u>, 지금은 잘 할 수 있어요.
유나: 마이클 씨는 한국말도 아주 잘 해요.
마이클: 아니에요. 한국말은 아직 잘 못해요.

Depending on the categories of words (or part of speech), this ~는데 connective has variants, as follows.

1 Adjective + (으)ㄴ데:
  형은 키가 <u>큰데</u> 동생은 키가 작아요. ← 크-다 big +ㄴ데 (형 older brother; 동생 younger sibling)
  동생은 키가 <u>작은데</u> 형은 키가 커요. ← 작-다 short + 으 + ㄴ데

2 Verb + 는데:
  형은 노래를 잘 <u>하는데</u> 동생은 노래를 잘 못해요.
  마이클 씨는 김치를 <u>좋아하는데</u> 토마스 씨는 김치를 안 좋아해요.

3 Adjective/verb (in past tense) + 는데:
  노래를 잘 <u>했는데</u> 지금은 잘 못해요.
  어제는 <u>추웠는데</u> 지금은 안 추워요.

[Practice]

Combine the two sentences using the connective ~는데 as shown in the example.

[Example]

마이클 씨는 축구를 좋아해요. 그런데 토마스 씨는 축구를 싫어해요.
→ 마이클 씨는 축구를 좋아하는데 토마스 씨는 축구를 싫어해요. (싫어하다 to dislike)

1 민지 씨는 한국 드라마를 좋아해요. 그런데 링링 씨는 한국 영화를 좋아해요.
  → _____.

2 제니퍼 씨는 커피를 마셔요. 그런데 미나 씨는 커피를 안 마셔요.
  → _____.

8 물어볼게요 I will ask her/him (about this).

In this section, we introduce ~(으)ㄹ게요. This structure expresses an action or intention of the speaker that will take place in the future. In *My Korean: Step 2*, we will learn the ways in which Koreans express details about the future or what we call "future tense" in Korean (i.e., [으]ㄹ 거예요). In general, the structure ~(으)ㄹ게요 indicates how the speaker (first person) will react or what he/she will do in response to what the other person has said as shown in the examples.

151

Part 3

Thomas needs help with his Korean homework.

토마스:　제니퍼 씨, 지금 바빠요?
민지:　　왜요?
토마스:　한국어 숙제가 어려워요.
민지:　　그럼, 제가 도와줄게요. Considering the situation, I will help you with your home-
　　　　work assignment

Michael and Minjee are at a Korean restaurant.

마이클:　이 식당은 뭐가 맛있어요?
민지:　　비빔밥이 아주 맛있어요.
마이클:　그럼, 비빔밥 <u>먹을게요</u>.
민지:　　저도요.

Michael is cooking Korean food.

민지:　　마이클 씨, 지금 뭐 하고 있어요?
마이클:　불고기를 요리하고 있어요? 그런데, 설탕이 없어요.
민지:　　그래요? 그럼, 설탕을 <u>사올게요</u>.
마이클:　감사합니다.

Michael wants to see if Minjee is available.

마이클:　민지 씨, 지금 시간(이) 있어요?
민지:　　지금 아주 바빠요. 그런데 왜요?
마이클:　아니에요. 다음에 다시 <u>올게요</u>. (다시 again)

　　Depending on the ending of the verbs, the vowel '으' is inserted before ~ㄹ게요 is attached
to the stem, as follows.

1　먹다 → 먹- + 으 + ㄹ게요 → 먹을게요 (Since the stem '먹' ends with a consonant, the vowel
　　is inserted.)
2　사오다 → 사오- + ㄹ게요 → 사올게요 (Since the stem '사오' ends with a vowel, ~ㄹ게요 is
　　added.)

Exercises

● **Complete the following dialogues with the choices given.**

[Example]

가 보세요; 먹어 보세요; 읽어 보세요; 해 보세요; 마셔 보세요

마이클:　미나 씨, 안녕하세요?
미나:　　마이클 씨. 안녕하세요?
마이클:　지금 어디에 가요?
미나:　　커피를 마시고 싶어요. 어디가 좋아요?

152

Lesson 7: Korean markets and college clubs 한인 마트와 대학 동아리

마이클: 그럼, 학교 앞 커피숍에 (1) _____. 라떼가 맛있어요.
미나: 감사합니다.

(커피숍 coffee shop; 라떼 latte)

토마스: 한국어를 잘 하고 싶어요. 어떻게 해요?
민지: 그럼, 매일 신문을 (2) _____.
토마스: 신문이요?
민지: 네, 저도 매일 신문을 읽어요.

(신문 newspaper)

제니퍼: 유나 씨, 어디 아파요?
유나: 아니요. 그냥 피곤해요.
제니퍼: 그럼, 매일 사과 주스를 (3) _____. 몸에 아주 좋아요.
유나: 그래요?

(피곤하다 to be tired; 매일 everyday; 사과 주스 apple juice)

● Answer the following questions in Korean using ~**고 싶어요** as shown in the example.

[Example]

오늘 저녁에 뭐 먹고 싶어요?
→ 오늘 저녁에 스파게티를 먹고 싶어요. (스파게티 spaghetti)

  4 이번 주말에 뭐 하고 싶어요?

       → _____.

  5 졸업 후에 (after graduation) 뭐 하고 싶어요?

       → _____.

  6 쇼핑몰 (shopping mall) 에서 뭐 사고 싶어요?

       → _____.

  7 방학 (school break) 에 어디에 가고 싶어요?

       → _____.

● Complete the following sentences by connecting two related parts.
  8   한국 음식을 먹으러   가. 은행에 가요
  9   편지를 부치러   나. 도서관에 가요
  10 커피를 마시러   다. 대사관에 가요
  11 비자를 받으러   라. 카페에 가요
  12 돈을 찾으러   마. 식당에 가요
  13 책을 빌리러   바. 우체국에 가요

● Complete the following sentences by connecting two related parts.
  • 주말에 영화를 같이   14 요리할 수 있어요?
  • 오늘 오후에 테니스를 같이 15 칠 수 있어요?

153

Part 3

- 불고기를   16   볼 수 있어요?
- 한국 역사책을   17   읽을 수 있어요?

● **Fill in the blanks with the best word from the options provided.**
[영화, 연극, 드라마, 음식, 무슨, 만날 수 있어요?, 마실 수 있어요?]

빌: 주말에 제니퍼 씨하고 같이 18 _____를 보고 싶어요?
제니퍼: 음, <미션 임파서블> 어때요? 저는 탐 크루즈를 아주 좋아해요.
빌: 저도 좋아요.
민지: 이번 토요일에 시간 있어요? 같이 식사해요.
마이클: 네, 시간 많아요. 19 _____ 음식을 먹고 싶어요?
민지: 음 . . .초밥하고 돈까스를 먹고 싶어요.
마이클: 그럼, 토요일 1시에 도서관에서 20 _____?
민지: 네, 좋아요.

Lesson 7: Korean markets and college clubs 한인 마트와 대학 동아리

Activity 1

My social network

친구들과 여러분의 사진에 대해서 이야기해 보세요. 소셜 미디어에 있는 여러분의 사진을 보여줄 수 있어요. 사진에 대해서 서로 물어보세요. You can show photos from your social media (e.g., Facebook, Instagram, and Twitter). Talk about them with classmates. Ask questions of each other about the photos.

이름 Name	언제 찍었어요? When was the photo taken?	어디에서 찍었어요? Where was the photo taken?	누구하고 같이 찍었어요? With whom did you take the photo?	여기, 이 사람이 누구예요? Look here. Who is this person?
(1) 윤호	지난 주말에 찍었어요.	멘도타 호수에서 찍었어요.	친구하고 같이 찍었어요.	제 여자친구예요.
(2)				
(3)				
(4)				
(5)				

Friends
Pixabay.com

Photos in social network
Pixabay.com

Part 3

Activity 2

Visiting local Korean markets

한인 마트가 어디에 있어요? 여러분이 사는 지역에 있는 한인 마트에서 한국 음식을 사 봅시다. 한국 음식에 대해서 친구들과 이야기해 봅시다. Where are Korean markets? Let's buy Korean food at a Korean market in your community. Let's share about the Korean food with classmates.

Vegetables in Korean Markets
Pixabay.com

이름 Name	뭐 샀어요? What did you buy?	한인 마트가 어디에 있어요? Where is the Korean market?
(1) 윤호	초코파이	시카고에 있어요?
(2)		
(3)		
(4)		
(5)		
(6)		

Lesson 7: Korean markets and college clubs 한인 마트와 대학 동아리

Cultural notes

Korean street food

Make sure to check out Korean street food on the Internet when you plan to travel around Korea! Korea is a foodie kingdom. You can eat lots of street food in every neighborhood at all times of the day. After shopping, sightseeing, and visiting historical sites, you can enjoy street food from carts or tents. Try *gim-bap* (김밥), *man-du* (만두), tornado potato (토네이도 감자), *dak-kko-chi* (닭꼬치), and a variety of fried snacks (튀김) from the street vendors.

Korean markets in the United States

Have you ever visited a Korean grocery store? If not, find a Korean grocery market (called 한인 마트 in Korean) near your neighborhood, where you will find various Korean (or Asian) ingredients and foods including prepared foods, ready-to-cook, marinated meats, Korean snacks, and much more. At some Korean grocery stores, after grocery shopping, you can enjoy some home-made Korean food in the food court area. On this website, you will find lists of Korean grocery stores and markets across the United States: www.maangchi.com/shopping/us. In some states, there is a giant Korean grocery chain called "H-mart," which is a super- or mega-style grocery market.

Student clubs and organizations

Do you want to learn something exciting outside of the classroom? You can find and develop your interests and potential abilities by participating in various student organizations. Lots of college students spend their free time participating in various club activities or student organizations in Korea. By engaging in activities with your classmates, you develop social skills, and have various cultural, and educational experiences. Take a few minutes to share your experiences with classmates. Are you a member of a club at your university? Which student organizations or clubs are you in?

Vocabulary expansion

여러분은 어떤 동아리에 참여하고 있어요? 여러분이 아래 동아리의 회장이라고 생각해 보세요. 친구에게 함께 동아리를 하자고 이야기해 보세요. What kind of student organization have you joined? Let's say you are the president of the following student organizations. Ask a friend to join the student organization.

Part 3

정보 Information	동아리 1 Student organization 1	동아리 2 Student organization 2
동아리 이름 name of the student organization	아름다운 손 Sign Language Club	노 젓는 날 Rowing Club
활동 activity	수화 sign language 병원 hospital 청각장애 hearing impairment 봉사활동 volunteer service	요트 yacht 배 boat 카누 canoe 노 젓기 rowing 수영 swimming
자격 qualification	1~3학년 freshmen–junior	모든 학년 all school years
모임 장소 meeting place	대학 병원 university hospitals	멘도타 호수 Lake Mendota
모임 횟수 number of meetings	주1번 once per week	주2번 twice per week

Students' group meeting 1
Pixabay.com

Students' group meeting 2
Pixabay.com

Translations of Dialogues I and II

Dialogue 1

Rachel: Yoon-ho, what are you eating now?
Yoon-ho: It's a Choco-pie. I bought it from a Korean grocery market. Try it. Here it is.
Rachel: Wow, it's delicious. Where is the Korean grocery market?
Yoon-ho: It's on Park Street. There is another one on University Avenue.
Rachel: Is that so? I didn't know that. I also want to buy a Choco-pie. Yoon-ho, can you go to the Korean grocery market with me today?
Yoon-ho: What should I do? I have an appointment today with a friend. I am going to Lake Mendota to take pictures with my friend from a student organization. Let's go together next time.

Lesson 7: Korean markets and college clubs 한인 마트와 대학 동아리

Rachel:	Is that so? Then, let's go there together next time. Next time, no matter what. Certainly!
Yoon-ho:	Okay. I am so sorry. Let's go there together next time, no matter what.

Dialogue 2

Yoon-ho:	Rachel, take a look at this picture.
Rachel:	What picture is it?
Yoon-ho:	It's the picture taken last weekend. I took it with my friend at Lake Mendota. Here, the one who is wearing glasses is my girlfriend.
Rachel:	Yoon-ho, do you have a girlfriend? Um . . . your girlfriend is very pretty. By the way, what is her name?
Yoon-ho:	It's Yuna. I met her first at the photography student organization. Are you involved in any student organization?
Rachel:	Yes I am. I am learning Taekwondo at a Taekwondo student organization. Taekwondo was very difficult at first but now it's very fun. But, actually, I want to learn Korean dance as well.
Yoon-ho:	There is one dance student organization, too. By the way, Yuna is the president of the dance student organization. I will ask her about it.
Rachel:	Ah, okay. Thank you.

Lesson 8

Studying Korean 한국어 공부하기

Learning goals

- Express reasons for actions.
- Make stronger suggestions.
- Use simple conditional clauses.

Grammar and expressions

- 한국어가 재미있어서 . . . Because Korean is so fun (to learn) . . .
- 열심히 하려고 해요. It is my intention to work hard.
- 대화를 많이 들으면 . . . If you listen to the dialogues many times . . .
- 연습하세요/연습하지 마세요. Please practice/Don't practice.
- 저는 한국에서 온 교환학생이에요. I am an exchange student who came from Korea.
- 한국 문화에 대해서 . . . About Korean culture . . .
- 저도요. Me, too.

Activities

- Ways of studying Korean
- Interviewing your friends

Part 3

Cultural notes

- Korean language programs in Korea
- What do you like to do with your Korean friends?

Vocabulary expansion

- Words for study skills

Lesson 8: Studying Korean 한국어 공부하기

DIALOGUE 1

Trying hard. 열심히 하려고 해요

Rachel talks about tips for learning Korean from Ling Ling who is taking the same Korean language course.

레이첼: 어머! 링링 씨, 안녕하세요?
링링: 레이첼 씨? 오랜만이에요! 잘 지냈어요?
레이첼: 네. 잘 지냈어요. 링링 씨는요?
링링: 저도 잘 지냈어요. 한국어 공부는 재미있어요?
레이첼: 네. 재미있어서 열심히 하려고 해요. 그런데 요즘 수업이 조금 어려워요.
링링: 그래요? 그럼 교과서의 CD를 자주 들어보세요. 대화를 많이 들으면 아주 좋아요.
레이첼: 아, 그렇구나! 저는 단어 공부가 참 어려워요.
링링: 무조건 외우지 마세요. 친구들과 함께 대화를 연습하세요. 그럼 대화를 잘 할 수 있어요. 그리고 대화도 쉽게 기억할 수 있어요.
레이첼: 고마워요, 링링 씨!

Word check-up

어머	(adv.)	exclamation; oh!
오랜만이에요.		Long time, no see. (오랜만 is a short form of 오래 간만)
지냈어요 (지내다)	(v.)	to pass/spend a day (past tense)
열심히 熱心-	(adv.)	hard/diligently
~하려고 해요		try to ~
요즘	(adv.)	these days, lately
어려워요 (어렵다)	(adj.)	to be difficult/challenging
교과서 敎科書	(n.)	textbook
대화 對話	(n.)	dialogue/conversation
그렇구나	(excl.)	I see.
단어 單語	(n.)	word/vocabulary
자주	(adv.)	frequently/often
들어보세요 (듣다)		try to listen to
무조건	(adv.)	unconditionally/unequivocally
연습하다 鍊習-	(v.)	to practice
기억하다 記憶-	(v.)	to remember
저절로		unconsciously/without knowing
외우다	(v.)	to memorize
쉬워요 (쉽다)	(adj.)	easy

DIALOGUE 2

I am studying Korean. 한국어를 공부하고 있어요

Rachel introduces Ji-Young, her language partner, to Yoon-ho. She also shares with Yoon-ho how they exchange ideas about their language and culture.

윤호: 레이첼 씨, 여기서 뭐 해요?

레이첼: 윤호 씨! 지금 지영 씨 하고 같이 한국어(를) 공부하고 있어요. 참, 지영 씨, 여기 윤호 씨(는) 제 친구예요.

지영: 안녕하세요, 전 한국에서 온 교환학생 김지영이에요. 레이첼 씨 대화 파트너예요. 레이첼 씨하고 같이 한국어를 연습해요.

윤호: 만나서 반가워요. 저는 이곳 대학교 경제학과 1학년이에요. 만나서 어떻게 공부해요?

레이첼: 지영 씨하고 같이 한국어 표현을 연습해요. 그리고 지영 씨가 숙제도 도와줘요.

지영: 레이첼 씨는 미국 문화에 대해서 가르쳐줘요. 그리고 영어도 가르쳐줘요.

레이첼: 앞으로 우리 셋이 자주 만나서 한국어로 이야기 해요!

윤호: 좋아요!

지영: 저도요!

Video clip

Lesson 8: Studying Korean 한국어 공부하기

Word check-up

교환학생 交換學生	(n.)	an exchange student
여기서		at/in here
온 (오다)	(v.)	to come
파트너	(n.)	partner
만나서 반가워요		nice to meet you.
이곳	(n.)	here, this place
1학년 1學年	(n.)	freshman
어떻게	(adv.)	how/how come
표현 表現	(n.)	expression
숙제 宿題	(n.)	homework/assignment
문화 文化	(n.)	culture
~에 대해서		about ~
도와줘요 (도와주다)	(v.)	to help
영어 英語	(n.)	English
가르치다	(v.)	to teach/to instruct
가르쳐줘요 (가르쳐 + 주다)		[spacing] to help some teach [something]
자주	(adv.)	often/frequently
앞으로	(adv.)	in the future/from now on
이야기해요 (이야기하다)	(v.)	to converse/talk with someone

Grammar and expressions

1   한국어가 재미있어서 . . . Because Korean is so fun (to learn) . . .

In Lesson 6, we've learned that ~어서/아서 connects two events sequentially, as shown here:

1   학교에 가서 공부를 해요. I go to school and then study (at the school).
2   친구를 만나서 영화를 봤어요. I met friends and then we watched a film.

In 1 the subject of the sentence sequentially connects the two events in the order of going to school and then studying. In 2 the subject meets his/her friends first, and then they (the subject and his/her friends) all go to a movie together.

In this section, we will introduce another usage of the structure ~어서/아서. When you elaborate reasons, conditions, or causes for the following actions or states, you may use the structure '~어서/아서'. This structure provides the reasons or justifications for the succeeding actions or states, and thus it is translated as "because, since, as . . ." Here are some examples:

3   한국어가 재미있어서 매일 한국 드라마를 봐요. ← 재미있 – (다) + ~어서
4   토마스 씨는 키가 커서 농구를 잘 해요. ← 키가 크 – (다) + ~어서
5   제니퍼 씨는 예뻐서 인기가 많아요. ← 예쁘 – (다) + ~어서 (인기가 많아요 someone is popular.)
6   수업에 늦어서 죄송합니다. ← 늦 – (다) + 어서 (늦다 to be late)
7   떡볶이를 많이 먹어서 배가 많이 불러요. ← 먹 – (다) + 어서 (배가 많이 불러요 the stomach is completely full.)

→ As shown, the first part (clauses) specifies the reasons or justification of the following part (clauses) and the two parts (or clauses) are connected with ~어서/아서.

165

Part 3

Here are sample dialogues between Jenny and Michael.

제니: 마이클 씨, 지금 뭐 해요?
마이클: '런닝맨'을 보고 있어요. (런닝맨 is a popular variety show in Korea)
저는: '런닝맨'이 너무 재미있어서 자주 봐요. (자주 often)
제니: 저도 '런닝맨'을 아주 좋아해요.
마이클: 제니 씨, 어디 아파요? (어디 아파요? Are you sick?)
제니: 아니요. 괜찮아요. 어제 잠을 못 <u>자서</u>, 좀 피곤해요. (괜찮아요 I'm fine; 잠을 자다 to have a good sleep)
마이클: 그럼, 이 '박카스'를 마셔요. (박카스 is an energy drink that is popular among Koreans and is similar to Red Bull in the United States)

[Practice]

Complete the following sentences.

1   오늘은 너무 바빠서 _____ .
2   수업에 늦어서 _____ .

   (수업에 늦다 to be late for class)

2   열심히 하려고 해요. It is my intention to work hard.

The structure verb stem + ~(으)려고 해요 expresses a situation or case where you want to "intend to do (something)." It can be translated as "it is my/his/her (= the speaker's) intention to do" or "the speaker (or the subject of the sentence) intends to do something." Here are some examples:

1   이번 방학에 한국에 <u>가려고</u> 해요. (← 가 – (다) + 려고 해요)
2   오늘 저녁에 중국 음식을 <u>먹으려고</u> 해요. (← 먹 – (다) + 으려고 해요)
3   이번 주말에 이 책을 다 <u>읽으려고</u> 해요. (← 읽 – (다) + 으려고 해요)
4   한국어가 너무 재미있어서 열심히 <u>하려고</u> 해요. (← 하 – (다) + 려고 해요)

→ Depending on the stem form i.e., ending with a vowel (e.g., 가 – ; 하 –) or ending with a consonant (e.g., 먹 – ; 읽 –), (으)려고 해요 is attached to the verb stem, accordingly.

Following are sample dialogues between Rachel and Jennifer using the structure ~(으)려고 해요.

레이첼: 이번 방학에 뭐 해요?
제니퍼: 한국어 공부를 열심히 <u>하려고 해요</u>.
레이첼: 어떻게 공부를 <u>하려고 해요</u>?
제니퍼: 한국 드라마를 매일 <u>보려고 해요</u>. (한국 드라마 K-drama; 매일 everyday)
레이첼: 지금 뭐 해요?
제니퍼: 한국 역사책을 읽고 있어요. (한국 역사 Korean history)
레이첼: 한국 역사책이요?
제니퍼: 네, 한국 역사가 너무 재미있어서 매일 한국 역사책을 <u>읽으려고 해요</u>.

With the past-tense 했어요, ~(으)려고 했어요 gives an interpretation of intended and yet unsuccessful event, as shown here:

5   여름 방학에 한국에 가려고 했어요. (I intended to go to Korea, but I didn't/couldn't go.)
6   전화를 하려고 했어요. (I intended to call you, but I couldn't.)

Lesson 8: Studying Korean 한국어 공부하기

3 대화를 많이 들으면 . . . If you listen to the dialogues many times . . .

The structure ~(으)면 . . . is used for simple conditional in subordinate clauses in Korean, and it is usually translated as "If . . ." as shown in the following examples.

1 비가 오면 집에서 음악을 들어요. (← 오 – (다) + 면) If it rains . . .
2 한국어 책을 매일 <u>읽으면</u> 한국어를 잘 할 수 있어요. (← 읽 – (다) + 으면)

   If you read a Korean book every day . . .

3 키가 <u>크면</u> 농구를 잘 할 수 있어요. (← 크 – (다) + 면) If you are tall . . .
4 몸이 <u>아프면</u> 병원에 가요. (← 아프 – (다) + 면) If you are sick . . .

The 으 – insertion in this structure depends on the forms of the stem; when the stem ends with a consonant, the vowel – 으 is inserted by default for the ease of pronunciation.

Given this, here is a dialogue between Yoon-ho and Rachel.

레이첼: 저는 한국어를 잘 하고 싶어요.
윤호: 그럼, 한국 드라마를 많이 보고 케이팝 (K-pop)을 많이 들으면 한국어를 잘할 수 있어요.
사라: 네, 저도 매일 한국 드라마를 보려고 해요. 그리고 한국 음악도 들으려고 해요.
윤호: 음, 그리고, 한국 남자친구가 있으면 한국어를 잘할 수 있어요.
사라: 네? 정말요?

4 연습하세요/연습하지 마세요. Please practice/Don't practice.

In order to express a direct, and yet, polite command or exhortation, the imperative form ~(으)세요 is used as shown here:

1 잘 들으세요. (← 듣 – (다) + 으세요) Please listen carefully.
2 이 책을 읽으세요. (← 읽 – (다) + 으세요) Please read this book.
3 여기 앉으세요. (← 앉 – (다) + 으세요) Please sit down here.
4 따라하세요. (← 따라하 – (다) + 세요) Please repeat (after me).

For negation, the imperatives use ~지 마세요 as in "don't do + verb." Here are the negative command forms of the verbs used earlier:

5 이 음악을 듣지 마세요/이 책을 읽지 마세요.
6 여기 앉지 마세요/저를 따라하지 마세요.

Here are example dialogues with this structure:

제니퍼: 한국어를 잘하고 싶어요.
유나: 그럼, 한국어 CD를 자주 들으세요. 그럼, 잘할 수 있어요. (듣 + 으세요 → 들으세요)
마이클: 쉿! 도서관에서 <u>이야기하지 마세요</u>. (쉿 hush)
민지: 아, 미안합니다.

5 저는 한국에서 온 교환학생이에요. I am an exchange student from Korea.

In this section, we are going to learn what we call the "noun-modifying form" ~(으)ㄴ + noun. It is difficult to translate this idea into English mainly because of the different tense systems between Korean and English. Let's focus on the form, first.

167

Part 3

1 한국에서 온 교환학생 ← 오 – (다) + ㄴ + noun (= 교환학생 exchange student)
2 호수에서 찍은 사진 ← 찍 – (다) + 은 + noun (= 사진 photo)
3 안경을 쓴 사람 ← 쓰 – (다) + ㄴ + noun (= 사람 person)
4 어제 먹은 불고기 ← 먹 – (다) + 은 + noun (= 불고기 bulgogi)

In Korean, the noun-modifying forms (i.e., the (으)ㄴ form) come before the nouns and modify the following nouns as shown. In terms of form, the structure combines verb stems with (으)ㄴ as in 온 (오 + ㄴ); 찍은 (찍 + 으 + ㄴ); 쓴 (쓰 + ㄴ); 먹은 (먹 + 으 + ㄴ). Then, it is placed just before the noun (i.e., 교환학생, 사진, 사람, 불고기). In terms of meaning, here are the closest translations in English:

5 한국에서 **온** 교환학생 the exchange student <u>who came from Korea</u>
6 호수에서 **찍은** 사진 the photo which I <u>took</u> at the lake
7 안경을 **쓴** 사람 the person who <u>put on (at some point in the past) and is now wearing</u> glasses
8 어제 **먹은** 불고기 the bulgogi (Korean-style barbecue) we <u>had</u> (or ate) yesterday

Here are sample dialogues with the noun-modifying forms used earlier.

마이클: 이거 무슨 사진이에요?
제나: 어제 멘도타 호수에서 <u>찍은</u> 사진이에요. (← 찍 - (다) + 은 + 사진)
다빈: 저기 안경을 <u>쓴</u> 사람은 누구예요? (← 쓰 - (다) + ㄴ + 사람)
탐: 제 여자 친구예요.
제니퍼: 어제 먹은 불고기가 어땠어요? (← 먹 - (다) + 은 + 떡볶이)
마이클: 정말 맛있었어요. 또 먹고 싶어요.

In relation to different tenses in Korean (i.e., present, past, and future), the noun-modifying form + [noun] can be complex as shown. But do not worry! We will gradually introduce this noun-modifying form again with examples in later chapters in this textbook series:

9 저기 **서 있는 남자** 가 누구예요? Who is that <u>man who is now standing</u> over there?
10 여기 **내일 읽을 책** 이 있어요. Here is <u>the book we will read</u> tomorrow.

"방가방가" 반가워요 [방가워요]

For ease of pronunciation, in general, the neighboring speech sounds affect each other, and thus the speech chain flows smoothly. Usually, the previous sounds will be more affected by the following sounds as we pronounce words or sentences. Using the specific example here, 반가워요 sounds like [방가워요] as the final nasal sound 'ㄴ' [n] is affected by the following consonant 'ㄱ' [k/g] and ends up sounding more like ㅇ [ng] in the syllable-final position. The reasoning behind this sound change is for ease of articulation (or pronunciation) such that the speaker can pronounce the words more easily and fluently.

Here are more examples:

한국 → [항국], 한강 (Han River) → [항강], 난간 (handrail) → [낭간]

6 한국 문화에 대해서 . . . About Korean culture . . .

Let's talk *about* Korean culture and lifestyle . . . The expression ~대해서 always follows nouns plus '~에' and it is translated as "regarding or about" the nouns. For instance, Tom is interested in Ji-Young and thus he wants to know more about her.

탐: 지영 씨에 <u>대해서</u> 알고 싶어요.
영미: 지영 씨에 <u>대해서</u>요? 지영 씨에 <u>대해서</u> 뭘 알고 싶어요? (뭘 is a contracted form of 무엇 + 을)

Lesson 8: Studying Korean 한국어 공부하기

탐: 지영 씨는 무슨 영화를 좋아해요? 지영 씨는 무슨 음식을 싫어해요? 지영 씨는 무슨 음악을 좋아해요?

영미: 탐 씨는 지영 씨에 대해서 정말 많이 알고 싶어해요.

탐: 네, 저는 지영 씨에 대해서 모두 알고 싶어요. (모두 everything)

[Practice]

What would you like to know more about?

Question: 무엇에 대해서 알고 싶어요?

1 한국 드라마에 대해서 알고 싶어요.
2 한국 영화에 대해서 알고 싶어요.
3 한국 음식에 대해서 알고 싶어요.
4 한국 역사에 대해서 알고 싶어요.
5 한국 이름에 대해서 알고 싶어요.

7 저도요. Me, too

Instead of repeating what has been said, in English we usually agree by saying "Me, too" or "The same here." In a similar manner, in Korean, we use the expression "저도요," which is a combination of "저 me," the particle "~도 also, too" and "~요 the sentence ending."

민지: 뭐 마시고 싶어요?
마이클: 아이스 커피요. (아이스 커피 iced coffee)
제니퍼: 저도요.
미나: 저도요.

How can we say (my majors) in Korean?

In Lesson 6, we talked about some popular majors at college. Here are more majors:

Economics 경제학	Political Science 정치학	Food Science 식품 영양학	Language Education 언어 교육학
Finance 재정학	Computer Engineering 컴퓨터 공학	Statistics 통계학	Mechanical Engineering 기계공학
Law/legal Studies 법학	Anthropology 인류학	American Studies 미국학	Philosophy 철학

Exercises

● Using the structure ~(으)려고 해요 complete the following sentences.
  1 내일은 시험이 있어서 _____ .
  2 지금 배가 고파요. 그래서 _____ .
  3 지금 배가 아파요. 그래서 _____ .
  4 한국어를 잘 하고 싶어서 _____ .

● Using the structure ~(으)면 complete the following sentences.
  5 _____ 병원에 가 보세요.
  6 _____ 매일 한국인 친구하고 이야기하세요.

169

Part 3

    7 _____ 인기가 많아요.
    8 _____ 집에서 비디오 게임해요.

- Answer the following questions using the structure ~고 있어요.
  9   지금 뭐 해요?
     → _____
  10 지금 뭐 먹어요?
     → _____

- As shown in the example, make imperative sentences using ~지 마세요.

[Example]

Image created by authors with pixabay image

→ <u>이야기하지 마세요.</u>

11

pixabay.com

→ _____ .

12

Image created by authors with pixabay image

→ _____ .

13

pixabay.com

→ _____ .

- Connect two relevant parts to complete the sentences.
  - 한국어가 재미있어서
  - 오늘은 날씨가 좋아서
  - 어제는 비가 와서
  - 마이클 씨는 키가 커서
  - 제니퍼 씨는 친절해서
  - 방이 깨끗해서 (방 room; 깨끗하다 to be clean)

14 소풍을 가고 싶어요. (소풍 picnic)
15 기분이 좋아요.
16 농구를 잘 해요
17 집에 있었어요.
18 친구를 잘 도와줘요.
19 매일 공부해요.
20 친구를 잘 도와줘요.

- **Translate the following sentences into English.**
  21 어제 먹은 음식은 불고기예요.
   → _____
  22 저기 키가 큰 남자는 김 선생님이에요.
   → _____
  23 여기 이 학생은 중국에서 온 교환학생이에요.
   → _____

Activity 1

Ways of studying Korean

여러분은 어떤 방법으로 한국어를 공부해요? 다음 중 여러분이 좋아하는 방법을 고르고 이유를 말해 보세요. What kind of study tools do you use when you study Korean? Choose one study tool from the following options and explain why you like that tool more than others.

레이첼: 한국어 공부가 너무 어려워요. Korean study is very difficult.
 윤호 씨는 한국어를 어떻게 공부해요? How do you study Korean?
윤호: 그럼 **교과서에 있는 CD를 자주 들어보세요**.
 Then why don't you listen to the CD in the textbook more often?
 CD를 자주 들으면 대화를 연습하는 데 도움이 돼요.
 If you listen to the CD more often, it helps you practice conversation.
레이첼: 아, 그렇구나! 저는 **한국 텔레비전 프로그램을 많이 봐요**.
 Ah, I see! I watch Korean TV programs a lot.
 그러면 **재미가 있어서 한국어 공부가 즐거워요**.
 Then it makes your Korean study enjoyable, because it's fun.
윤호: 좋은 생각이네요! 고마워요. That's a good idea! Thank you.

Video clip

Part 3

Activity 2

Interviewing your friends

Step 1

두 명이 한 조를 만들어요. 오른쪽의 질문을 보고 서로에 대해서 인터뷰해요.
Make a team of two people. Using the questions given, interview your partner.

Step 2

다른 조를 만나서 서로 소개해요. 다른 사람에게 여러분의 조원들을 소개해 주세요.
표를 완성하세요.
Meet other teams, and introduce your team members to them. Your partner will introduce you to the other teams, and you will introduce your partner to them. Fill out the following charts after meeting other teams.

제 친구의 이름은 _____예요/이에요. My friend's name is _____.	
(1) 이 도시에 언제 이사왔어요? When did he/she move to this city?	
(2) 취미가 뭐예요? What are his/her hobbies?	
(3) 가족이 몇 명 있어요? How many family members does he/she have?	
(4) 주말에 보통 뭐 해요? What does he/she usually do during the weekend?	
(5) 어디를 여행했어요? Where has he/she traveled?	
(6) Your own question?	

172

Cultural notes

Korean language programs in Korea

There are many popular Korean universities that offer Korean language programs at a variety of levels depending on your language ability and background in Korean. There are many benefits to learning Korean in Korea. First, you can choose to take diverse courses, including Korean history, literature, politics, society, environment, mass media, arts, etc. Second, if you attend Korean classes at a university in Korea, you have a more flexible schedule. So you can make friends with other Korean students and experience Korean culture off campus. Third, living in Korea allows you to better understand Korean culture and life since you become familiar with the local contexts.

What do you like to do with your friends?

Making friends means that you may have the same or similar views to share with someone or you may do things together with them. It makes you feel good when you spend time with your friends. To become a good friend to someone, you should know them better and also open yourself more to them. As a way of doing that, ask the following questions in Korean to your Korean friends:

1 시간이 있으면 뭐해요? When you have time, what do you do?
2 동아리에 대해서 이야기해요. Let's talk about your student organization.
3 가족에 대해서 이야기해요. Let's talk about your family.
4 무슨 음식을 좋아해요? What kinds of food do you like?
5 어느 나라를 여행하고 싶어요? Which country would you like to visit?

Vocabulary expansion

공부와 관련된 단어들에는 무엇이 있을까요? 다음의 단어들을 사용해서 여러분이 요즘 어떻게 공부하는지 설명해보세요. Which vocabulary is related to study? Let's explain how you study using the following vocabulary.

Vocabulary

읽다 *to read*

소리내서 읽다 to read out loud
마음 속으로 읽다 to read to yourself
읽어보다 to try to read

기억하다 하다 *to remember*

기억이 가물가물하다 memory is foggy
기억력이 (안)좋다 (not) good memory
외우다 (= 암기하다) to memorize

쓰다 *to write*

받아쓰다 to dictate
요약(要約)하다 to summarize
지우다 to erase/delete

Part 3

말하다 *to speak*

대화하다 to have a conversation
또박또박 말하다 to speak clearly
발표하다 to present

Translations of Dialogues I and II

Dialogue 1

Rachel: Oh! Ling Ling, hello!
Ling Ling: Rachel? Long time no see! How have you been?
Rachel: I have been good. What about you, Ling Ling?
Ling Ling: I have been good as well. Are you enjoying studying Korean?
Rachel: Yes. I am trying to study hard because it is fun. But these days, the class is a little difficult.
Ling Ling: Is it? Then try listening to the CD in the textbook often. It's very good to listen to the dialogues a lot.
Rachel: Ah, I see! For me, studying vocabulary is very difficult.
Ling Ling: Do not memorize the words by rote. Practice the dialogue with your friends. Then, you will be good at speaking Korean and you can remember the dialogue easily.
Rachel: Thank you, Ling Ling!

Lesson 8: Studying Korean 한국어 공부하기

Dialogue 2

Yoon-Ho: Rachel, what are you doing here?

Rachel: Uh, Yoon-Ho! I am studying Korean with Ji-Young. Oh, Ji-Young, this is Yoon-Ho, my friend.

Ji-Young: Hello, I am an exchange student from Korea, Ji-Young Kim. I am Rachel's conversation partner. I practice Korean with her.

Yoon-Ho: Nice to meet you. I am a freshman in Economics here. How do you study when you two meet?

Rachel: I practice the expressions I learned from Korean class with Ji-Young, and Ji-Young helps with my vocabulary and homework.

Ji-Young: Rachel teaches me about American culture, and she teaches me English as well.

Rachel: The three of us should meet often in the future and have a conversation in Korean!

Yoon-Ho: Sounds good!

Ji-Young: I agree.

Index

Note: Page numbers in italics indicate figures and page numbers in bold indicate tables on the corresponding pages.

"A and B" 124–125
About Korean culture . . . 168–169
activities: "Are you Michael?" 41; inquiring about food 60; interviewing your friends 172; introducing classmates 42; introducing favorite foods 59; Let's play Yut 134; Let's talk about weather around the world 112; My dating plan 1 94; My dating plan 2 95–96; My social network 155; poster fair 76; role play: Thanksgiving Day 132–133; visiting local Korean markets 156; ways of studying Korean 171; weekly class schedules 77; writing a letter 113
addressee terms 40
adjectives (or descriptive verbs) 106–107
adverbs, negative 109
alphabet, Korean see Hangeul
also/too 54
~and ~and 110–111
and/then 55–56
Are you available? Do you have free time? 86
Are you available to go with me? 145–146
aspiration rule 24

Because Korean is so fun (to learn) . . . 165–166
bowing 43
by the way 73–74

calendar, Korean 125–127
Chosun Dynasty 12
Christmas 136

Chuseok 125–128, 132–133
college clubs/student organizations See Korean markets and college clubs/student organizations
combinations of vowels and consonants 16–17
Coming back from Thanksgiving dialogue 119–120, 136
compound consonants, pronunciation of 22–23
compound vowels 17–18
conditional clause 10, 161
Confucianism 13
connecting dissimilar concepts with 는데 150–151
connecting nouns 124–125
connectives, sentence 150–151
consonants 11, 12–13; 14 basic Korean 15; combined with vowels 16–17; double 18–19; in *Hangeul* 13–14; pronunciation of syllable-final 20–22
conversational form 51
copular verb 37counting numbers 56–58, 57
counters 56–58; for time 89
cultural notes: Chuseok 125–128, 132–133; how to say "thank you" 114; Korean currency, "won" 96; Korean greetings 43; Korean home remedies 114; Korean language programs in Korea 173; Korean street food 157; Korea-Yonsei varsity games 96; K-pop 78; ordering food in Korean 61–62; universities in Korea 78;

Index

What do you like to do with your friends? 173
currency, "won" 96

dating 81–82; Are you available? Do you have free time? 86; cultural notes 96; Do you have time? 82–83; How much is it? Here it is 92–93; I want to go with . . . 90; My dating plan 1 activity 94; My dating plan 2 activity 95–96; My phone number is . . . 91–92; vocabulary expansion 97; What time is it? 86–89; What time is the game? 90; Where are you now? 84–85, 92
days of the week in Korean 126–127
demonstratives 52
descriptive verbs 106–107
destination particle 55
dialogues: Coming back from Thanksgiving 119–120, 136; Do you have time? 82–83; Do you know? 66–67; Hello? 31–32; How about? 68–69; I am learning Taekwondo 143–144, 158–159; I am studying Korean 164–165, 175; I don't feel well 105–106, 116; I'm American 33–34; I'm hungry 47–48; Shall we? 121–122, 137; Today's weather is so nice 103–104, 116; Trying hard 163, 174; What's this? 49–50; Where are you now? 84–85; Wow, it's delicious 141–142, 158–159
double consonants 18–19
Do you have time? dialogue 82–83
Do you know? 66–67
Do you like . . .? 52

expression for capability or ability 145–146
expression for encouragement 145
expression for intention 166
expression for speaker intention 151–152
expressions for wearing in Korean 148–149
express reasons 10, 161

favorite foods, introducing 59
fluent reading of words and sentences 23–24
future tense 9, 139, 151

go some places with certain purposes 147–148
grammar and expressions: "A and B" 124–125; About Korean culture . . .

168–169; adjectives (or descriptive verbs) 106–107; also/too 54; ~and ~and 110–111; and/then 55–56; Are you available? Do you have free time? 86; Are you available to go with me? 145–146; Because Korean is so fun (to learn) . . . 165–166; counting native-Korean numbers in 56–58, 57; destination particle 55; Do you like . . .? 52; Hello 34, 35–36; How do you say ____ in Korean?/In Korean, we say 123–124; How much is it? Here it is 92–93; I am . . . 36–37; I am an exchange student from Korea 167–168; I am learning Taekwondo 149–150; I am wearing glasses 148, *149*; If you listen to the dialogues many times . . . 167; I know/I don't know 70; irregular verbs 73; *Is* 안녕하세요 *a question? How do we respond?* 34–35; It is my intention to work hard 166; It was difficult at first but . . . 150–151; I want to . . . 71–72; I want to go with . . . 90; I will ask her/him (about this) 151–152; making a verb past tense 108–109; Me, too 169; My phone number is . . . 91–92; negative adverbs 109; Nice to meet you 37–38; noun + 는/은요? 109–110; noun + (이)요 70–71; In order to take pictures, we went to a lake 147–148; Please practice/Don't practice 167; questions 35–36; sentence ending 107–108; subject particle 53–54; This is my friend 38–39; Try kimchee 144–145; verbal conjugation 50–52, 70; very useful expressions 75; by the way, however; therefore, thus 73–74; What country are you from? 39; What is this? What is that? 52–53; What is your name? 36; What is '씨' for? 39–40; What kind of food? 122–123; What shall I do? (=There is nothing I can do about it) 147; What time is it? 86–89; What time is the game? 90; Where are you now? 92; Where is the math class? 74–75; Why don't you take a Korean class? 72; Yes and No 35
greetings 29–30; bowing in 43; cultural notes 43; Hello? 31–32, 34–35; I am . . . 36–37; I'm American 33–34; Nice to meet you 37–38; This is my friend 38–39;

Index

vocabulary expansion 43–44; What country are you from? 39; What is your name? 36; What is '씨' for? 39–40; Yes and No 35–36

Hallyu 78
Hangeul 11; 14 basic consonants in 15; combinations of vowels with consonants in 16–17; compound vowels in 17–18; double consonants in 18–19; fluent reading of words and sentences in 23–24; pronunciation of compound consonants in syllable-final position in 22–23; pronunciation of syllable-final consonants in 20–22; quick history of 12–13; syllable-final consonants in 20; ten basic vowels in 14–15; vowels and consonants in 13–14
Hangeul Proclamation Day 135–136
health *see* weather and health
Hello? 34–35; dialogue 31–32; phone conversations and 92
holidays 134–135
home remedies, Korean 114
horizontal vowels 16–17
hot and spicy rice cake 61–62
How about? 68–69
How do you say _____ in Korean?/In Korean, we say 123–124
however 73–74
How much is it? Here it is 92–93

I am . . . 36–37
I am an exchange student from Korea 167–168
I am learning Taekwondo 149–150; dialogue 143–144, 159
I am studying Korean dialogue 164–165, 175
I am wearing glasses 148, *149*
I don't feel well dialogue 105–106, 116
If you listen to the dialogues many times . . . 167
I know/I don't know 70
I'm American dialogue 33–34
I'm hungry dialogue 47–48
In Korean, we say 123–124
In order to take pictures, we went to a lake 147–148
inquiring about food 60

Interviewing your friends activity 172
intonation, statement, question 35
irregular verbs 73
ㄷ-irregular verbs 73
르-irregular verbs 70
Is 안녕하세요 *a question? How do we respond?* 34–35
It is my intention to work hard 166
It is shaped like a crescent-moon 128–129
It was difficult at first but . . . 150–151
I want to . . . 71–72
I want to go with . . . 90
I will ask her/him (about this) 151–152

Jiphyeonjeon 12

kinship terms 40
Kong-na-mul-guk 114
Korean alphabet *see Hangeul*
Korean markets and college clubs/student organizations 139–140; Are you available to go with me? 145–146; cultural notes 157; exercises 152–154; I am learning Taekwondo 143–144, 149–150, 159; I am wearing glasses 148, *149*; It was difficult at first but . . . 150–151; I will ask her/him (about this) 151–152; My social network activity 155; In order to take pictures, we went to a lake 147–148; Try kimchee 144–145; in the United States 157; Visiting local Korean markets activity 156; vocabulary expansion 157–158; What shall I do? (=There is nothing I can do about it) 147; Wow, it's delicious 141–142, 158–159
Korean street food 157
Korean words for majors 124
Korean words for majors II 169
Korea-Yonsei varsity games 96
K-pop 78

Let's play Yut activity 134
Let's talk about weather around the world activity 112
linking rule 23
location particle 74–75

markets, Korean *See* Korean markets and college clubs/student organizations

Index

Me, too 169

meals and foods 45–46; also/too 54; and/then 55–56; counting native-Korean numbers in 56–58, **57**; cultural notes 61–62; destination particle 55; Do you like . . .? 52; I'm hungry 47–48; subject particle 53–54; verbal conjugation 50–52; vocabulary expansion 62–63; What is this? What is that? 52–53; What's this? 49–50

months of the year in Korean 125–126

My dating plan 1 activity 94

My dating plan 2 activity 95–96

My phone number is . . . 91–92

My social network activity 155

nasal assimilation rule 24

native-Korean numbers 56–58, **57**, 87; calendar and 125–127; phone numbers and 91–92; telling time using 87–89

negative adverbs: 안 vs. 못 109

Nice to meet you 37–38

noun + 는/은요? 109–110

noun + (이)요 70–71

noun-modifying forms 167–168

numbers, native-Korean 56–58, **57**; calendar and 125–127; phone numbers and 91–92; telling time using 87–89

object particles 86

particle meaning "also/too" 54

past tense verbs 108–109

Please practice/Don't practice 167

possessive form 38

present progressive ~고 있어요 149–150

pronunciation: resyllabification 109

questions 35–36

reason or justification with ~어서/아서 165–166

re-syllabification rule 23

role play: Thanksgiving Day activity 132–133

Sam-gye-tang 114

school life 65–66; cultural notes 78; Do you know? 66–67; How about? 68–69; I know/I don't know 70; irregular verbs 73; I want

to . . . 71–72; noun + (이)요 70–71; poster fair activity 76; very useful expressions 75; vocabulary expansion 78–79; by the way, however; therefore, thus 73–74; Where is the math class? 74–75; Why don't you take a Korean class? 72

Sejong, King 12, 135–136

sentence connectives 150–151; "and/then" 55–56; "by the way/however; therefore, thus 73

sentence ending 107–108; ~지요 vs. ~어/아요 146; ~아요 vs. ~네요 107–108

Seol-reong-tang 114

sequentially connected with 어서/아서 129–130

Shall we? dialogue 121–122, 137

Shall we play a game? 130

simple conditional ~(으)면 167

Sino-Korean numbers 88–89

street food, Korean 157

student organizations *See* Korean markets and college clubs/student organizations

studying Korean 161–162; About Korean culture . . . 168–169; Because Korean is so fun (to learn) . . . 165–166; cultural notes 173; exercises 169–171; I am an exchange student from Korea 167–168; I am studying Korean 164–165, 175; If you listen to the dialogues many times . . . 167; interviewing your friends activity 172; It is my intention to work hard 166; Me, too 169; Please practice/Don't practice 167; Trying hard 163, 174; vocabulary expansion 173–174; ways of studying Korean activity 171

structure for suggestion or invitation 130

subject particle 53–54

suggestions 9–10, 65, 72, 117, 161

syllable-final consonants 20; pronunciation of 20–22; pronunciation of compound consonants in 22–23

syllables 12–13

Thanksgiving Day and Chuseok 117–118; "A and B" 124–125; Coming back from Thanksgiving dialogue 119–120, 136; cultural notes 125–133; How do you say _____ in Korean?/In Korean, we say 123–124; role play activity 132–133; Shall we? dialogue 121–122, 137;

Index

vocabulary expansion 134–136; What kind of food? 122–123

thank you 114

therefore 73–74

This is my friend 38–39

thus 73–74

time particle 90

Today's weather is so nice dialogue 103–104, 116

Trying hard dialogue 163, 174

two events sequentially connected 129–130

universities in Korea 78

verbal conjugation 50–52, 70

verbs: descriptive 106–107; irregular 73; made past tense 108–109

vertical vowels 16–17

Visiting local Korean markets activity 156

vocabulary expansion: dating 97; Korean markets and college clubs/student organizations 157–158; meals and food 62–63; occupations 43–44; school life 78–79; studying Korean 173–174; Thanksgiving Day and Chuseok 134–136; weather and health 114–115

vowels 11, 12–13; combined with consonants 16–17; compound 17–18; in *Hangeul* 13–14; ten basic Korean 14–15

Ways of studying Korean activity 171

weather and health 101–102; adjectives (or descriptive verbs) 106–107; ~and ~and 110–111; cultural notes 114; I don't feel well 105–106, 116; Let's talk about weather around the world activity 112; making a verb past tense 108–109; negative adverbs 109; noun + 는/은요? 109–110; sentence ending 107–108; Today's weather is so nice 103–104, 116; vocabulary expansion 114–115; writing a letter activity 113

weekly class schedules activity 77

What country are you from? 39

What did you do on Chuseok? 127–128

What is this? What is that? 52–53

What is your name? 36

What is '씨' for? 39–40

What kind of food? 122–123

What shall I do? (=There is nothing I can do about it) 147

What's this? dialogue 49–50

What time is it? 86–89

What time is the game? 90

When is Chuseok? 125–127

Where are you now? 84–85, 92

Where is the math class? 74–75

Why don't you take a Korean class? 72

won (currency) 96

Wow, it's delicious dialogue 141–142, 158–159

Writing a letter activity 113

Yes and No 35–36

Yu-ja-cha 114

Yut (game) 130, 134

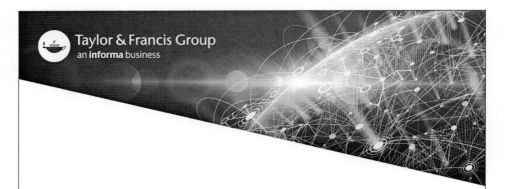

Taylor & Francis eBooks

www.taylorfrancis.com

A single destination for eBooks from Taylor & Francis with increased functionality and an improved user experience to meet the needs of our customers.

90,000+ eBooks of award-winning academic content in Humanities, Social Science, Science, Technology, Engineering, and Medical written by a global network of editors and authors.

TAYLOR & FRANCIS EBOOKS OFFERS:

- A streamlined experience for our library customers
- A single point of discovery for all of our eBook content
- Improved search and discovery of content at both book and chapter level

REQUEST A FREE TRIAL
support@taylorfrancis.com